The Sixth Patriarch's

Dharma Jewel Platform Sutra

六祖大師法寶壇經

Translated from the Chinese of Zongbao
Taishō Volume 48, Number 2008

D1481514

Buddhist Text Translation Society

2014

The Sixth Patriarch's Dharma Jewel Platform Sutra.

Newly translated from the Chinese by the Sixth Patriarch Sutra Translation Committee of the Buddhist Text Translation Society: Rev. Bhikshu Heng Sure (certifier), Yuh-chirn Liang, Allen Huang, Yi-huan Shih, Madalena Lew, and Martin J. Verhoeven.

©2014 Buddhist Text Translation Society
    Dharma Realm Buddhist University
    Dharma Realm Buddhist Association
    4951 Bodhi Way, Ukiah, CA 95482
    www.buddhisttexts.org
    www.drbu.org
    www.drba.org

First edition (Hong Kong) 1971
Second edition (USA) 1977
Third edition (USA) 2002
Fourth edition (USA) 2014

Buddhist Text Translation Society
4951 Bodhi Way, Ukiah, CA 95482

Library of Congress Cataloging-in-Publication Data

Huineng, 638–713.
    [Liuzu da shi fa bao tan jing. English]
    The Sixth Patriarch's Dharma jewel platform sutra : Liuzu da shi fa bao tan jing / translated from the Chinese of Zongbao.—Fourth edition.
        pages cm.
    "Taisho Volume 48, Number 2008."
    "Translated from the Chinese by Buddhist Text Translation Society."
    ISBN 978-1-60103-070-2 (alk. paper)
    1. Zen Buddhism—Early works to 1800. I. Hsüan Hua, 1908–1995, writer of supplementary textual content. II. Verhoeven, Martin, editor. III. Huineng, 638–713. Liuzu da shi fa bao tan jing. IV. Buddhist Text Translation Society. V. Title.

BQ9299.H854L613 2014
294.3'927—dc23

2014015324

Printed in the United States of America on acid-free, archival-quality paper.

Contents

Acknowledgements   vii

Editorial Note   ix

Preface by Tripitaka Master Hsüan Hua   xi

Translators' Introduction   xiii

MAP: The Places the Master Visited   lxxvi

MAP: Tang Prefectures in 741 (Hartwell)   lxxvii

A General Introduction by Bhikshu Fahai   1

CHAPTER ONE   Where It All Began   7

CHAPTER TWO   Prajna   23

CHAPTER THREE   Doubts and Questions   37

CHAPTER FOUR   Concentration and Wisdom   45

CHAPTER FIVE   Sitting Meditation   51

CHAPTER SIX   To Repent and Renew   53

CHAPTER SEVEN   Lively Encounters   65

CHAPTER EIGHT   Direct and Gradual   89

CHAPTER NINE   Imperial Summons   99

CHAPTER TEN   Final Instructions   103

A Brief Account of the Life of
   the Venerable Master Hsüan Hua   119

The Venerable Master Hsüan Hua's Eighteen Great Vows   127

Chinese Sutra Text (六祖大師法寶壇經)   133

Acknowledgements

The Committee wishes to gratefully acknowledge the many people whose talents and dedication inspired and sustained this new translation of *The Platform Sutra*. First, we wish to recognize the pioneering efforts of the early Buddhist Text Translation Society who introduced the first edition of this text in 1971 (Hong Kong), and the second edition in 1977 (San Francisco). The present translation would have been considerably more difficult without their groundbreaking efforts.

The primary responsibility for this new endeavor belongs to Rev. Heng Sure and Martin Verhoeven who were able to collaborate on the text for nearly a year due to the quiet support provided them by the Berkeley Buddhist Monastery in Berkeley, California. Their work immeasurably benefited from the support of a Chinese language team consisting of Yuh-chirn Liang, Allen Huang, and Yi-huan Shih who did all the painstaking background research and cross-checking of sources indispensable to accurate and informed translation work. They tirelessly documented the historical background of the sutra, sifted through conflicting accounts, and confirmed all the facts, as far as they can be ascertained, in any work of this antiquity. Moreover, they called our attention to the special Buddhist terms and linguistic subtleties of Chinese usage—all of which greatly enhanced the new English version. To them also fell the demanding task of character-by-character comparison between differing versions of this text, as well as proofreading, editing, collating and incorporating all the revisions made along the way.

A second level of close reading and cross-checking was provided by Yuen-lin Tan, and again by members of a Sixth Patriarch Sutra Seminar held at Dharma Realm Buddhist University in the Fall of 2013. Those participating in the seminar were Heng Jie Shi, Jin Shao Shi, Jin Lian Shi, Huali Yuan, James Roberts, Ernie Waugh, and Stacy Chen. The committee also benefited from insights on the Chinese Tripitaka from Dharma Master Heng Yun, the stylistic suggestions of Kuo Jin Vickers, the Sanskrit-to-Chinese research of Lauren Bausch, and the publishing advice of David Rounds.

For the Tang dynasty map "The Places the Master Visited" we need to thank Laura Tan for her careful rendering and design. And for the "Tang Prefectures in 741" map we are indebted to Prof. Peter K. Bol and Merrick Lex Berman, both at the Center for Geographic Analysis at Harvard University, for generously sharing their time and cartographic materials.

We would like further to thank the following: Stan Shoptaugh for the book design and layout; Toni Minor and Ilona Bray for English proofreading and copy-editing; Dharma Master Heng Yin who oversaw and expedited the Library of Congress filing; and, Anne Cheng for her work in assuring the publication of this book. Special appreciation is extended to Professors Henry Rosemont, Michael Nylan, and Ed Yee both for their scholarly advice on the Sisyphean task of coming up with dynamic English equivalents for key Chinese philosophical concepts, and for their encouraging us to see this project through to the end, these challenges notwithstanding.

Finally, we are forever indebted to our teacher, Master Hsüan Hua, who tirelessly lectured on the Buddhist classical texts daily, and who encouraged his students to learn the languages and to cultivate the character necessary for translating both the letter and the spirit of these sacred works.

Editorial Note

A number of explanatory and interpolated materials appear in both the Chinese text and its English translation:

1. Glosses, which appear within parentheses and in italics, indicate explanatory notes, comments, and insertions either made by the original compiler, or by subsequent writers, and which have been over time incorporated as a standard feature into the Zongbao Taisho text.

2. Words or phrases within brackets indicate the translators' editorial interpolations inserted either to clarify certain passages or to bridge the often wide gaps in continuity that inhere in a particularly terse text such as *The Platform Sutra*.

3. Italicized words and phrases indicate either technical terms (Sanskrit) or pinyin romanization.

4. Footnotes, all of which are supplied by the translators to aid the reader in understanding critical Buddhist technical terms or ideas.

Two versions of *The Sixth Patriarch's Sutra* are most widely available today: this one, the Zongbao text, dating from the Yuan dynasty (1271–1368); and an earlier and briefer manuscript, called the Dunhuang text. The work translated here has come to be known simply as the Zongbao in reference to the Chinese monk by that name who compiled it in 1291. It is a more mature version of the Dunhuang text, being longer by close to 10,000 characters. The Zongbao (Taisho Vol. 48; Number 2008) was incorporated into the Ming tripitaka and remains the most popular and widely used edition to date.

This translation also includes a prefatory introduction attributed to a Buddhist monk, Fahai, of the Tang dynasty (618–906). In some versions, Fahai's preface is inserted into an Appendix at the end of the sutra. Here, it is placed at the beginning, preceding Chapter One. It was this version, taken from Fahai's text collected in Roll 915 of the *Quantangwen* (全唐文) that our teacher, Master Hsüan Hua, lectured on at Gold Mountain Monastery in the late 1960s.

Preface

by Tripitaka Master Hsüan Hua

All of the sutras are guides to use in cultivating the Way. They may be delivered by Buddhas, Bodhisattvas, Patriarchs, and also by Arhats, spiritual incarnations, and gods. Though the doctrines within them vary, they all serve the same purpose.

The sutras delivered by the Buddha were translated from the Indian languages into Chinese, and thus they found their way into Chinese culture and society. In China, then, all of the sutras are translations, with the sole exception of this present work, *The Sixth Patriarch's Dharma Jewel Platform Sutra*, which is the recorded teachings of the great Chinese master, the Sixth Patriarch. The great Master was originally an illiterate peasant. When he heard this sentence of *The Diamond Sutra*, "Let your mind be unattached, clinging to nothing," he experienced an awakening, and went to Huangmei to draw near to the Fifth Patriarch, the great Master Hongren. The Fifth Patriarch bequeathed the wondrous Dharma to him, 'the mind certifying the mind,' which had been handed down in an unbroken succession from Patriarch to Patriarch. The Sixth Patriarch inherited this 'mind-seal' Dharma teaching, and proceeded to carry on the wisdom life of the Buddha, through his teachings, *The Platform Sutra*.

Now it has been translated into English, and the 'mind-seal' Dharma teaching of the Buddha has thereby been transmitted in perpetuity to the West. It is hoped that Westerners will now read, recite, and study it, and that they all will become Buddhas, Bodhisattvas, and Patriarchs. This is the main purpose of this translation. May all who read and hear it quickly realize the Buddha's Way.

Wherever this Sutra takes root, the proper Dharma may be found there as well, enabling living beings to directly realize Buddhahood. Such is the importance of this new translation. The Sutra is indeed a treasure trove; it is the true body of the Buddha, the compassionate mother and father of all living beings. It can give birth to limitless Buddhas, Bodhisattvas, and Patriarchs! May all in the West, who now read this sutra gain awakening and realize the Buddha's Way!

The sutras embody the precious wisdom of the Buddha. There are some, let us call them "academic sophists" who claim *The Shurangama Sutra* is not a teaching of the Buddha. This is most certainly not true, and so I have made the following vow: "If *The Shurangama Sutra* is false, may I fall into the unceasing hells forever."

Chang Baishan Seng
San Francisco
August 1977

Translators' Introduction

The teachings that the Sixth Great Master used to expound were all the complete direct message of the Great Vehicle; that is why this is called a 'sutra.' Its words are everyday, but its guidance is far reaching; the expression is easy, the meaning is clear. Everyone who reads it gets something from it. Master Mingjiao praised it by saying, "Those whose natural potentials are sharp will get the deep, and those whose natural potentials are dull will get the shallows." How true these words are!

—from Zongbao's "Afterword" of the 1291 Edition of *The Platform Sutra*

OVERVIEW

After the Fifth Patriarch, Hongren, had passed on the robe and bowl to the Sixth Patriarch, Huineng, he told him to immediately go into hiding. Huineng's life might be in danger, the Fifth Patriarch warned. The Sixth Patriarch fled, but was quickly pursued by an evil crowd wishing to steal these symbols of the Dharma's bequeathal. The first to catch up with him was a monk named Huiming, a rough and coarse-natured former military commander. Unable to wrest the items away by force, Huiming cried out, "Cultivator, cultivator! I have come for the Dharma, not for the robe." The Sixth Patriarch told him to calm down, and then instructed him on the essentials of Dharma: your own mind in its original purity and stillness is the Buddha. Huiming felt he had now at last received the 'secret meaning.' Yet its purport was so simple and straightforward that he asked further, "Other than the secret words and secret meaning you just uttered, is there yet *another* secret meaning?" The Master answered, "What I just told you is not a secret. If you look within yourself, you'll find the 'secret' is with you."

Less than a year earlier when Huineng, the Sixth Patriarch to be, first visited his teacher, the Fifth Patriarch Hongren, the Master asked him, "Where are you from? What do you seek?" Huineng replied, "Your disciple is a commoner from Xin Province in Lingnan. I come from afar to bow to you, and seek only to be a Buddha, nothing else." To test him, the Patriarch said, "If you are from Lingnan, you must be a barbarian. How could *you* become a Buddha?!" But Huineng replied, "People may come from the north, or come from the south, but fundamentally there is no north or south to the buddha-nature. The body of a barbarian and that of a High Master are not the same, but what difference is there in our buddha-nature?"

This initial intuitive understanding, so strikingly evident in the Sixth Patriarch even before he commenced formal study and received training, would later mature into the platform of his entire teaching—called the "direct teaching" (*dun jiao* 頓教). He succinctly conveyed its central tenet as follows:

> You should now believe that the knowledge and vision of the Buddha is just your own mind; there is no other Buddha. . . . Why don't you immediately see, right within your own mind, the true reality of your original nature?

Here then, in these two encounters we find the essence of the Sixth Patriarch's philosophy, and indeed the substance of the Buddha's teaching: all beings have the buddha-nature; all can become Buddha. As the Patriarch himself pointed out, "This teaching has been passed down from sages of the past; it is not my own wisdom." But what exactly is this "nature?" And how is it realized?

The Sixth Patriarch insists that this nature (*xing* 性), called the essential-nature or original-nature (*zi xing* 自性; *ben xing* 本性), is universally possessed by all sentient beings. It is not greater in the sage, or less in the average person. Human nature is the buddha-nature; Buddhas come from people. The difference between a Buddha and an ordinary living being, between the liberating joy of wisdom and the anguish of delusion, is one of degree, not of kind. In a fully awakened being, the nature is perfectly realized. In an ordinary person, this capacity lies dormant, covered over, and asleep, so to speak.

> You should know that the buddha-nature is fundamentally no different for the foolish and the wise. The only difference between them is: the foolish are confused; the wise are awakened.

Buddhas and living beings are two forms of a single substance, just as water and ice belong to a common element. In yet another example of the direct teaching, the Sixth Patriarch tells his followers:

> Good and Wise Friends, unawakened, Buddhas are just living beings. At the moment they awaken, however, living beings are Buddhas. Therefore, you should realize that the ten thousand dharmas are all within your own mind.

The fundamental sameness of the human and Buddha, the worldly and world-transcending, the ordinary mind and the Buddha mind are all different ways of expressing a corollary axiom of this teaching: "non-duality" (*bu er* 不二). In his very first formal lecture the Sixth Patriarch states unequivocally: "the Dharma of the Buddha is a non-dual Dharma." The fundamental sameness of a Buddha and an ordinary person also means that Buddhahood is not a future state or a far-distant celestial abode, but exists "right within your own mind" and is immediately available. The implications are manifold.

When taken together, we are presented with a powerful and re-sounding totalistic vision of human nature as the buddha-nature, unconditioned by culture, schooling, gender, ethnicity, or even religious belonging. It is not even delimited by time and space, nor by birth or death. This indwelling capacity remains whole and complete within all of us, waiting to be fully expressed if only we could see it.

> Our real nature is non-dual. It is not diminished in ordinary people, nor is it greater in worthy sages. It is not disturbed amid the afflictions; nor is it stilled and static while in chan concentration. It does not end, nor endure forever. It does not arrive or leave; and has no location: neither inside nor outside nor in the middle. Unborn, undying, its essence and appearance is 'just so; as it really is.' It is permanent and unchanging—it is called the 'Way.'

The ideas of innate and primary wholeness, non-duality, and immediacy form the unvarying thematic core of the Sixth Patriarch's teaching career and color all of his talks and encounters.

Three interrelated themes flow from this direct teaching.

First, because the awakened nature is intrinsic to all beings, it cannot be sought for outside (*bu cong wai ru* 不從外入).

Thus, the compound characters (*kai wu* 開悟 lit. 'opening up') meaning "awakening" suggest a releasing of what has been there all along, much as a flower opens to or unfolds in the sun. Rather than an acquisition of something novel, divine, or even transcendent, awakening connotes a natural enlivening of an immanent and inborn human capacity. In describing the path to awakening, the text avoids language hinting at mysticism, or any sense of striving, acquiring, obtaining, getting, or even having an experience. Instead, it favors a single term, "seeing" (*jian* 見) to convey the experience, which could also be rendered as "realizing" or "waking up to." One is being led to behold something intrinsic and at-hand all along, rather than to yearn for a dreamy transcendent reward somewhere beyond.

Indeed, it was in the here-and-now, in the midst of his everyday routine while standing in front of a village shop that Huineng, then a poor woodcutter, had his own initial awakening. Upon hearing a stranger utter the famous line of text from *The Diamond Sutra*: "Let your mind be unattached, clinging to nothing," his mind immediately opened (*xin ji kai wu* 心即開悟). Mere months later he arrived at an even deeper understanding upon hearing the same line, this time recited by his teacher, Hongren. The Sixth Patriarch relates, "As soon as these words were uttered I experienced a profound awakening, and understood that the inherent nature embraces the ten thousand things." He exclaimed,

> *How unexpected! The essential nature is intrinsically pure.*
> *How unexpected! The essential nature is originally unborn and undying.*
> *How unexpected! The essential nature is complete in itself, lacking nothing.*
> *How unexpected! The essential nature is fundamentally still and unmoving.*
> *How unexpected! From the essential nature the myriad dharmas come to be.*

Master Hongren, the Fifth Patriarch, affirmed Huineng's realization, and as if to further emphasize the point, told him: "To study the Dharma without recognizing your original mind is useless. If you recognize your original mind, and see your essential nature, you can be called 'a great hero,' 'a teacher of gods and humans,' a 'Buddha.'"

In this terse exchange we see the subtle and dynamic relationship between student and teacher that the direct teaching requires. This pedagogy is sometimes called the "mind pointing to the mind," because the insights and profound understanding (Skt. *prajna*) that awakening occasions are intrinsic and cannot properly be transmitted or transferred from one person to another. Because the true mind (*zhen xin* 真心) is in itself complete, nothing can be added to it by a teacher. Its subtle, wondrous functioning (*miao yong* 妙用) must be discovered, or more accurately, recovered, in and by oneself. The essential nature is in itself unconditionally whole and ever-present. Its origins and ends are left unstated and unexplained. The original nature just is—not created *ex nihilo*, nor ever destroyed (*bu sheng mie* 不生滅). Thus, the teacher can implant nothing in it, or even impart anything to it. Teaching is limited to nurturing and drawing out its innate fullness. When the student "sees," the teacher simply acknowledges or affirms the achievement. And when the student understands its use, the teacher sends the student on his or her way. The teacher's job is finished once the student knows the Way.

The only words often spoken between the master and disciple at this point are "thus it is." This phrase attests to what is ever and always so by using the lightest of allusions: "thus; as it really is." In 1948 when Master Hsuan Hua traveled to Nanhua monastery to bow to Ven. Xuyun (虛雲 'Empty Cloud') who was then 109 years old, such a mutual recognition occurred. Of their meeting Master Hua simply wrote:

> *The noble Yun saw me and said, "thus it is."*
> *I saw the noble Yun and affirmed, "thus it is."*
> *The noble Yun and I, both 'thus,'*
> *Universally vow that all beings will be 'thus' too.*

A corollary expression goes, "Before one is awakened, ten thousand words are not enough; after one is awakened, even a single word is too much."

In this tradition, the goal of the skillful spiritual teacher (Skt. *kalyanamitra*; Ch. *shan zhi shi* 善知識) is not to inculcate the student with a prescribed body of knowledge, but to stimulate the student to self-knowledge. As a result, the teaching style tends less to profess or preach than to provide situations that can spur the student to self-recognition and rouse direct insight. The teacher does not bestow the vision, but only presents the student with the means to discover it within. This earnest and sustained transformative activity of direct inquiry, self-reflection, and maturing in the Way is called self-cultivation (*xiu xing* 修行). As the dynamic nature of the Chinese characters imply (修 lit. 'correcting; repairing; to rectify' and 行 lit. 'steps;' 'walking') self-cultivation requires a total mind-body engagement; it is a 'doing,' a way of becoming an exemplary person, which entails both rigorous training and an active 'pruning' and 'repairing' of one's character and conduct. Chapter Seven, "Lively Encounters," a record of the actual face-to-face encounters between the Sixth Patriarch and his closest disciples, vividly illustrates this method.

This leads to the second theme: the need to engage, to practice, to enact (*xing* 行). Although our original nature is the Buddha-nature, most of us could not describe our present state as Buddhahood. The Sixth Patriarch's question posed above is straightforward, not merely rhetorical: "Why don't you immediately see, right within your own mind, the true reality of your original nature?" He answers with an analogy drawn from the natural world, "It is like when thick clouds obscure the sun; if the wind doesn't blow, the sun cannot shine."

The "clouds" are the self-inflicted impediments of delusion and afflictions (Skt. *klesa*) which we have let cover over our fundamental pure nature. They obscure our vision so that we are unable to "recognize our own mind and see our nature." Huineng develops this analogy more fully,

> It is like the sky above which is always clear, and the sun and moon which are ever bright. Even if they are obscured by floating clouds that overshadow the world below in darkness, the sky above remains clear. If a wind suddenly comes up, scattering the clouds, then above and below are both bright, and everything reappears and becomes visible. The tendency of people is to constantly drift like the clouds in the sky.
>
> Good and Wise Friends, insight is like the sun, and wisdom is like the moon. Insight and wisdom are always bright, but if we attach to external things, the floating clouds of errant thoughts cover over our essential nature so it is obscured and cannot shine.

The Dharma, when practiced, acts like wind scattering the clouds.

According to the Sixth Patriarch, the Dharma teachings are something to be used (*yong* 用), applied and tested. Indeed, for the Master, the Way must be walked, or it is not the Way. The *dao*/Way elucidated by the Sixth Patriarch is not a religious doctrine, nor an ontological or metaphysical Truth, nor even a faith to espouse. The Chinese character for the Way (*dao* 道) denotes movement, literally 'walking' (走, 辶), suggesting the Way is existentially real, found underfoot. As the word implies, a 'path' is for walking, and reveals itself only in and through the traversing of it, *in vivo* not *a priori*. Confucius may have been hinting at something similar in saying, "It is the person that can make the Way great, and not the Way that can make the person great." (*Analects* 15:28)

Thus the Way is discovered concretely, not surmised abstractly. Stationary, there appears to be no Way, but as soon as one walks, the road appears. Hence the saying, "From afar, the mountain appears unscalable, but when you get to the bottom of the mountain, there is always a way." This point cannot be overemphasized: without 'walking' there is no Way. Without serious and sincere engagement, the true path falls away and disappears from sight; or perhaps worse, descends into a dead end of clever debate, (*ko tou chan* 口頭禪; lit. 'head-mouth zen'). As Huineng stresses to his followers, "This must be practiced with the mind; not merely recited by the mouth. Verbal repetition without mental cultivation is like a fantasy, a hallucination, as dew drops and a lightning flash." The poet-cultivator Han Shan (c. 9th century) eloquently conveyed the same sentiment in a verse from his Cold Mountain writings:

> *Talking about food won't make you full,*
> *babbling about clothes won't keep out the cold.*
> *A bowl of rice is what fills the belly;*
> *it takes a suit of clothing to make you warm.*
> *And yet, without stopping to consider this,*
> *you complain that Buddha is hard to find.*
> *Turn your mind within! There he is!*
> *Why look for him outside?*

Just as eating satisfies hunger, and wearing clothes fends off the elements, only self-cultivation quickens one's inherent wisdom. The Sixth Patriarch berates those who speak of wisdom with their mouths but harbor delusion in their minds. He warns,

> Good and Wise Friends, people chant "prajna" all day long
> without realizing the prajna of their own essential nature.
> Just as talking about food will not satisfy hunger, so too only

talking about emptiness, even for myriad eons, will give
you no insight into your own nature—ultimately it is of no
benefit.

Similar expressions appear throughout the Buddhist tradition, for example the sayings: "the thousand mile journey begins with a single step," or the following student teacher exchange: "Where is the Buddha?" "Your own mind is the Buddha;" and, "Where is the Great Way?" "It is the ground right under your feet." Nor is this sentiment unique to East Asia. The American poet, Emily Dickinson, voiced an almost identical notion in describing the spiritual not as a distant goal, but a here-and-now way of being. As she wrote, "So instead of getting to heaven, at last—I'm going, all along."

The Sixth Patriarch's explication of the Way is completely consistent with the overarching motif of the text: non-duality. The Dao, the Dharma, are not presented as the results of philosophical conjecture or as divine revelations bequeathed from without, but as signifiers of living truths residing within. Or to use a Chan expression, the teachings are "fingers pointing to the moon." While traveling, the Sixth Patriarch encounters a nun who constantly recites *The Mahaparinirvana Sutra*, but nonetheless does not understand some of its finer points. As the Master begins to explain a passage for her, she inquires about specific characters in the scroll, and the Master replies, "I cannot read the words; please ask about the meaning." The nun exclaims, "If you cannot even read the words, how can you understand the meaning?!" The Master answers, "The subtle meaning of all Buddhas has nothing to do with words and language."

The Sixth Patriarch in fact tells his students, "All Buddhas of the past, present, and future, as well as the twelve divisions of sutras are originally inherent, whole and complete, within human nature." He goes so far as to maintain that, "If there were no people in the world, all the myriad Dharma-teachings would not exist by themselves." As with wisdom (Skt. *prajna*) and awakening (Skt. *bodhi*), so too with the teachings (Dharma): they are of a piece with the mind, and firmly grounded in human nature. Self-understanding is the key to unlocking the meaning of the Sutras because the essential nature is the very wellspring of the teachings themselves. Memorizing and reciting Sutras, as an act of devotion is admirable, but alone cannot bring liberation. This can be accomplished only by tilling and cultivating the ground of the mind (*xin di* 心地), the inner landscape; in other words, by "seeing your nature."

When Fada, an early disciple, first meets the Sixth Patriarch, his pride keeps him from fully bowing in respect. When the Master asks him to explain his breach in etiquette, Fada boasts that he has memorized a lengthy scripture, and that, "I have recited *The Lotus Sutra* over three thousand times already!" The Master replies, "It doesn't matter if you recited it ten thousand times. If you understood the Sutra's meaning, you would not be so overbearing, and might be a fellow cultivator with me. You have applied effort in vain, yet don't even understand how wrong you are." The Master then instructs him that confusion and awakening are in the person, not magically in a text. He cautions, "If your mouth recites and your mind practices, you 'turn' the Sutra; but if your mouth recites while your mind does not practice, then the Sutra 'turns' you."

In the mind-ground approach of the Sixth Patriarch, the scriptures of *sutras, shastras,* and *vinaya* (the 'three baskets,' or Tripitaka) are to be used, not simply worshipped. Translating Dharma (*fa* 法) as "Law" completely misses this key point: the Dharma teachings are tools for self-discovery, not canonical writ. They are intended as mirrors of and for the human mind, as catalysts for change, not merely as icons of devotion or incantatory prayer. Only because of people is there Dharma. Huineng tells his students,

> All the sutras and writings were established because of people—and could only have been set up because of [their] wisdom nature. . . . Therefore, you should realize that the myriad Dharma-teachings arise because of people, and all Sutras are taught and explained for people.

But how does one attain the Way? How are we to uphold the Dharma teachings? This brings us to a third theme in the text: setting up nowhere, (*wu suo zhu* 無所住); attaining nothing-to-attain.

The Sixth Patriarch must direct his students to truths that cannot be grasped, cannot be seen, cannot be thought, and yet are more real than anything that can be held, seen, or imagined. He faces the same paradox the Buddha faced: how to elicit in his students a certain intellectual stance, an open-minded sensibility that avoids falling into the two extremes of eternalism or nihilism. For example, when one of his disciples asks about the 'impermanence' of our passing thoughts and the 'permanence' of our essential nature, the Master pointedly contradicts the established teaching by answering in the opposite: it is the Buddha-nature which *is impermanent*, and the confused mind which *is permanent*. The student is stunned. But then Huineng explains,

> Don't you realize—if the buddha-nature were permanent, then what good or bad states would there be to speak of? And not a single person until the end of time would ever aspire to bodhi. That is why I say it is impermanent. This is precisely the path to true permanence taught by the Buddha. Moreover, if all things were impermanent, then everything

would have its own nature which was subject to birth
and death, and the truly permanent nature would not be
universal, all-pervading. That is why I say they are permanent.
And that is precisely what the Buddha meant by teaching
true impermanence.

It could not have been an altogether pleasant and comfortable
experience to sit at the Master's feet. As a doctor pokes and prods to
diagnose and heal, the Master as a spiritual physician upbraids, challenges, probes for hidden faults, and exposes petty ways and venal
tendencies that cover over each student's inherent wisdom. At one
point he even describes his method as, "*Good medicine is bitter to
the taste/Good advice often hurts the ears.*" Yet, beneath the stern, im-
posing exterior one finds a deeply caring and compassionate 'father-
teacher,' who presses his students precisely because life is short, and
our time in this world is of the essence. Do not waste either because,
as he warns, "a frantic passage through life will end in bitter regret."
A certain compassionate urgency, an edge, can be found in his tone,
not unlike the elder in *The Lotus Sutra* parable who desperately pleads
with his unaware children to put down their toys and escape from
a burning house. In describing the Buddha's reason for coming into
the world, the Master is perhaps relating his own,

It is only because living beings cover over their own light
with lust and craving for sensory experiences, become
enslaved to things outside and disturbed within, that the
World Honored One is roused from his samadhi to exhort
them to cease, to not seek outside themselves, and instead
to realize they are the same as the Buddha. . . I, too, am
always exhorting people to realize the Buddha's knowledge
and vision within their own minds. But ordinary people

> are perverse; confused and deluded, they do wrong. Their
> talk may be good, but their minds are bad. Greedy, hateful,
> envious, fawning and flattering, deceitful, and arrogant, they
> take advantage of others and harm living creatures. Thus,
> they only realize the knowledge and vision of living beings.

Finally, as this last passage shows, it is not lack of esoteric knowledge or metaphysical insight that impedes our enlightenment, but our lack of self-understanding. The most ordinary of human faults, character flaws, and bad habits obscure our "seeing" and obstruct our liberation. So too, it is only by facing up to and correcting these "afflictions" that the Buddha of our own mind is found. That is the meaning of the Sixth Patriarch's enigmatic statement: "the afflictions themselves are bodhi; they are non-dual and not different" (*fan nau ji shi puti* 煩惱即是菩提, *wu er wu bie* 無二無別).[1]

There may indeed be heavenly realms but they will be found only by traversing the ground right under one's feet. There may be devas and gods, but they are irrelevant to one's own liberation. Moreover, to dream of ethereal paradises, or to seek escape from the world through drugs and hedonistic indulgence, or even to attempt to "leave it all behind" through hermit-like withdrawal—all are utter folly, according to the Master. *This* world is the field of awakening; one's *own* person is the raw material of Buddhahood. Looking elsewhere for liberation and happiness will only compound our dissatisfaction and angst. The further one travels, the less one knows. To illustrate, the Master gives a verse:

---

1 Chinese *fan nao* 煩惱; Skt. *klesa*; inclinations and tendencies, often lying deep in the mind, that cause mental, emotional, and physical distress and agitation. They hinder practice and obstruct awakening. They are rendered under a wide range of names: 'afflictions,' 'defilements,' 'hindrances,' 'yokes,' 'outflows,' 'raging streams,' 'fetters,' 'arrows,' 'jungle,' 'entanglement.'

The Buddha Dharma is right here in the world,
There is no awakening apart from this world;
To search for Bodhi somewhere beyond this world,
Is like looking for a rabbit with antlers

For the Sixth Patriarch all time is one time, all places are one place. When it comes to self-cultivation, only the here-and-now matter. Time and again, the text brings us back to the immanent, the immediate, and to the most unexpected place one might look for the Buddha: our own mind. This very mind is the Buddha (*fo ji shi xin* 佛即是心), and what is directly and immediately in front of us is the entirety of the Dharmarealm. This mind, this thought, this moment is the only ground of awakening (Skt. *bodhimanda*). As Master Hsüan Hua wrote, "The ten dharmarealms are not beyond a single thought."

And yet a certain quandary confronts us when we try to attend to the here-and-now, and to appreciate the urgency of the moment. For not only is the past gone and unrecoverable, and the future not yet come and out of reach, but the present moment, too, does not really exist and cannot be seized. The present is, as Huineng tells us, "empty and still." In his final words to his most devout students, he emphatically reminds them,

> The Way is pure, pristine, and unmarked. All of you be careful
> not to "contemplate pure stillness" or a vacant mind. The
> mind is fundamentally pure; with nothing to grasp or reject.

Non-abiding, no fixed phenomenon, nothing that can be held on to—all of this is in the very nature of things. Such a radical insistence on the fleeting, transient, and insubstantial nature of all things, even the present moment itself, might suggest despair. But Huineng is no philosophical nihilist. He would undoubtedly consider himself a realist—facing things as they truly are. Moreover, he insists, only in emptying out this apparent or 'false' emptiness can we discover true existence. The emptiness he expounds echoes the emptiness presented in *The Heart Sutra* through Avalokitesvara who upon "seeing the emptiness of things immediately crossed beyond all suffering and difficulty." Contrary to what one might expect, true emptiness opens into wondrous existence, not dispirited gloom.

Our basic nature, according to the Sixth Patriarch, is non-attachment, and it blossoms only when it flows freely, clinging to nothing. To be "empty" is to be free of insecurity, anxiety, and a gnawing sense of lack. Buddhist emptiness paradoxically then must be read not as dark extinction but as a light-filled fullness of existence. Knowing that "there is not a single thing that can be obtained" leads not to the dead-end it might portend, but to an unexpected flourishing of unencumbered freedom, joy and wisdom. No doubt, this unanticipated fruit of emptiness—liberated knowing and seeing—partly helps explain Huineng's repeated exclamation upon his own awakening: "How unexpected! How unexpected!"

The physicist, J. Robert Oppenheimer, found this puzzling truth to be at the heart of modern scientific observation, and a large part of why Buddhism attracted him. He wrote,

> If we ask, for instance, whether the position of the electron remains the same, we must say 'no;' if we ask whether the electron's position changes with time, we must say 'no;' if we ask whether the electron is at rest, we must say 'no;' if we ask whether it is in motion, we must say 'no.' The Buddha has given such answers when interrogated as to the conditions of man's self after his death; but they are not familiar answers for the tradition of seventeenth and eighteenth-century science.

The Sixth Patriarch does not condemn grasping, craving, and wanting as immoral or evil. The tone of the text throughout is largely descriptive, not judgmental. He simply points out that such unquenchable thirst (Skt. *trsna*) does not deliver. Craving, as the Buddha observed, only brings suffering, stress, and dissatisfaction (Skt. *dukkha*). The restless seeking, the "frantic passage through life" as Huineng calls it, covers over people's light to such a degree that they "become enslaved to things outside and disturbed within." In a lengthy and graphic teaching to the monk Zhidao, the Master says,

> You should know that the Buddha [taught] because deluded people mistook the combination of the five skandhas for their own essence and being, and discriminated so as to make all things external to themselves. They loved life and dreaded death, drifted and flowed along from thought to thought, unaware that this was all an unreal dream, hollow and false. They pointlessly turned round and round on the wheel of birth and death, wrongly imagining that the eternal bliss of nirvana was some kind of suffering, and all day long frantically sought after something else.

The "direct teaching" arises as a compassionate response to human stress and suffering. Its directness is in part a response to the gravity of what *The Lotus Sutra* calls "the one great matter"—birth and death—and the need to speak the unvarnished truth regarding it. Huineng's teaching, like the Buddha's, has one goal: to exhort people to stop and rest, not to seek outside themselves, and realize that the "knowledge and vision of the Buddha is just their own mind." He urges on his disciples by quoting a line from *The Vimalakirti Sutra*, "just here and now, regain your original mind." He then empowers them with the following:

Good and Wise Friends, when I was with the Venerable
Master Hongren, I awoke as soon as I heard his words and
immediately saw my original nature as it truly is. That is why I
am conveying this teaching and practice, so that students of
the Way may directly awaken and realize Bodhi. Each of you
look into your own mind; see your original nature yourself.

One important and common misimpression, however, needs to
be discussed. The Sixth Patriarch's philosophy is often depicted as exclusively self-directed ('self-power,' *zi li* 自力), requiring no beliefs or
faith (*xin* 信), as opposed to other-reliant dependence ('other-power,'
ta li 他力). This characterization is overdrawn and not entirely accurate. First, in Huineng's understanding, a distinction between 'self-
power' and 'other-power' sets up a false dichotomy. The Dharma of
non-duality means that the Buddha and the living being, one's own
pure mind and the Pure Land of Amitabha, are fundamentally the
same. The full and proper use of one's own mind *is* the Buddha's
mind. Huineng is most explicit on this:

If your essential nature is balanced and centered, the living
being is a Buddha. When your essential nature deviates off
course, the "buddha" is a living being. If your mind is devious
and crooked, the "buddha" is concealed within the living
being. But with one thought balanced and trued, the living
being becomes a Buddha. Our own mind itself holds the
Buddha, and this inherent Buddha is the real Buddha. If our
own mind did not have its own inherent Buddha, where
could the real Buddha be sought?

Faith is not absent from his teachings; it is simply recessed. Or, to
be more precise, faith is so implicit and deep-seated in *The Platform
Sutra*'s narrative that it might be overlooked.

Faith, for Huineng, is a natural quality of the awakening; it is integral to, rather than a substitute for, true seeing. Thus, it does not require a blind acceptance of something external, or dependence on someone else, but instead an appreciation of one's own abilities. Conversely, lack of faith would not indicate an atheistic disbelief in the Buddha, but an underestimation of one's own worth. Thus, a better rendering of *xin* (信) in this sutra might be "trust" or "confidence." It grows from an intuitive appreciation of the soundness of the essential nature, and an affirmation of one's own ability to walk the same path the Buddha walked. The 'faith' Huineng exhorts his students to embrace is not in him, nor even in the Buddha, but within themselves. He says, "Your own mind is the Buddha. Never doubt this!"

The direct teaching, to and from the nature, can be seen again when the Sixth Patriarch ritually initiates new students to Buddhism through the formal 'taking refuge' ceremony. Taking refuge in the Buddha, in Huineng's teaching, is not a leap of faith into the arms of a divine being who saves you, but a personal commitment to 'saving' yourself (*du* 度; lit. 'cross over;' and related to *du* 渡 'ferry across'). He tells the initiates,

> Good and Wise Friends, each of you examine yourself. Do not go about this incorrectly. The sutra [Avatamsaka] clearly says you should return and rely on your own Buddha, not with some other Buddha. If you do not return to the Buddha within, there is nothing you can rely on.

The self-reliance that Huineng encourages should not, however, be construed as hubris or arrogance. Instead, it is something more tentative and open to continuous self-examination, rubbing and polishing. Moreover, faith is not final, an end in itself. Rather it is, like all of the Sixth Patriarch's 'dharma-doors,' instrumental: a means to an end; provisionally useful but not ultimately secure. Clinging to anything, even to faith, will invariably become an impediment. Trust in the essential nature then would be rewarded not with 'salvation,' as in religious doctrine, but with direct understanding, or *gnosis*. One could easily picture the Master saying, "Before awakening, one believes; after awakening, one knows."

CENTRAL ELEMENTS & THEMES

While a number of versions of *The Platform Sutra* exist, it is noteworthy that most renditions rather closely parallel one another, and show sufficient similarity in content and themes to suggest they derive from a common source, however obscure to us now. Central elements might be delineated as follows:

The Essential Meaning of All Buddhas . . .

The text itself traces its lineage back to what it calls the "source" (*yuan* 原), not of a particular school, as the character *zong* 宗 is often narrowly translated, but to the source teachings (*zong zhi* 宗旨) of all Buddhas. This grounding of the text's deep-rooted purport is witnessed by the listing of successive teachers given in the final chapter. Here, having been asked how many generations have passed along this teaching since its beginnings, the Sixth Patriarch enumerates a patriarchal lineage going back not just to the Buddha of our era, Shakyamuni, but to seven Buddhas of antiquity that preceded him. In fact, the Patriarch says, the number of Buddhas who have passed along this teaching is "numberless and incalculable." In other words, this "source teaching" holds the essential meaning of all Buddhas, and as such is without beginning or end. In cultivating it, one is not simply following a particular Buddha, or even following in the footsteps of all Buddhas, but is actually seeking after what they sought. Huineng exhorts his students:

> To learn the Way, look within, observe your own essential nature;
> Then you are one and the same with each and every Buddha.

The Way is to be sought not in the past or in the future, but right now in oneself. When he finally grasped this point, Zhichang, one of the Master's students, exclaimed: "*Our own nature is the essential source of awakening.*"

Transformative Not Merely Informative . . .

The text can seem doctrinally elusive. This, however, may be less by default than by design. If the source teaching holds that one's own nature is the ground of awakening, and that people's original nature is from the outset pure, still, and in itself whole and complete—in short, that *this* very mind is Buddha —then any "teaching" by definition could only be an expedient device to stimulate one's innate understanding.

That would explain why the *content* of the teaching is so masterfully embedded in its *conveyance.* *What* is being taught is inseparable from *how* it is taught. Insight and understanding happen only by actively moving from one place to another—here, from confusion to awakening. The student does not get hold of the teaching; rather, the teaching gets a hold on the student. Learning is transformative, not merely informative.

Doctrinal meaning thus is not static, fixed, and absolute, but rather, fluid, flexible, and catalytic. As the Sixth Patriarch explains, there are only different kinds of people, not different kinds of Dharma. There seem to be 84,000 diverse teachings only "because people have 84,000 kinds of affliction." Dharma is not Dharma unless it 'works,' that is to say, appropriately serves to convert the afflictions (Skt. *klesa*) into insight, liberation, and an end to suffering. As with chemical catalysis, the Dharma teaching acts merely as an agent of change; it 'dissolves and releases.' Once the desired transformation occurs, the teaching can, indeed *must*, be let go of.

A corollary to this understanding is that no method of practice, or vehicle of deliverance (*cheng* 乘), is inherently better than another. Superiority or inferiority is not intrinsic (within the thing itself), but instrumental (determined by effectiveness; appropriate to the person). Thus, the Sixth Patriarch admonishes a student seeking to debate the longs and shorts of the different "vehicles" within Buddhism,

> Vehicles are methods of practice; not subjects for debate.
> Cultivate yourself; don't ask me. At all times, your own
> essential nature is itself "truly as it is."

The opportune and pragmatic nature of the Teaching (Skt. *upaya*) helps us understand the seemingly enigmatic expression: "the emptiness of dharmas." All vehicles, like all dharmas, are *empty* (Skt. *sunya/sunyata*; Ch. *kong* 空). As in the famous Parable of the Raft, the Sixth Patriarch views all the texts and methods of practice ("Dharma doors" *fa men* 法門) only as expedient conveyances and temporary supports. All are equally means to an end, not ends in themselves. In the Raft Parable, the Buddha tells of a traveler who encounters a vast stretch of water, dangerous on this side and safe on the other. There is no boat to ferry him across. So he cleverly "gathers grass, wood, branches and leaves to make a raft, and with the help of the raft crosses over safely to the other side, exerting himself with his hands and feet." Once safely on the other shore, the man wisely beaches the raft and abandons it, instead of foolishly carrying it on his back and head wherever he goes.

The raft is a metaphor for the Buddha's teachings, the Dharma. The Buddha concludes, "In the same manner, O bhikkhus, I have taught a doctrine similar to a raft—it is for crossing over, and not for carrying (lit. 'getting hold of'; *graha*, 'to grasp'). You, O bhikkhus, who understand that the teaching is similar to a raft, should give up even good things (Skt. *dhamma*); how much more then should you give up evil things (Skt. *adhamma*)."[2]

For the Sixth Patriarch, even the notion of "this shore" and "the other shore" would likely pose a false dichotomy. Non-duality implies that only a single thought, not a vast body of water, separates samsara from nirvana. From the primary position, samsara *is* nirvana; the afflictions themselves *are* bodhi. To the awakened mind there is no getting and nothing to attain. Even coming or going, birth and death lack borders. Here, things present truly as they are (*zhen ru* 真如); and as *The Avatamsaka Sutra* says, "one place is every place; and one time is all time." A change of mind *is* the other shore; one arrives but there is no moving, just still quiescence. Thus in his instructions to disciple Zhicheng, the Master says, "Awaken by yourself to your own essential nature; awaken directly by cultivating directly. There are no gradual stages; nor anything to set up. All things are still and empty."

The philosophy of the Sixth Patriarch consequently can seem at times almost meandering and inaccessible. It might be better deemed *peripatetic*, 'traveling from place to place,' or in this case, from one person to another, thus illustrating another facet of non-dwelling (*wu suo zhu* 無所住). Rather than a fixed "school" with a set curriculum, the peripatetic teaching takes place while walking, and in the Buddhist sense, *in* walking. The Dharma comes alive only in the actual taking up of the practice of "going back to the root; returning to the source"

2 from *Majjhima-nikaya*. (Pali Text Society, pp. 134–35). Also, *Alagaddupama Sutta*; MN 22.

(*yong* 用). Practice activates meaning; cultivation and understanding mutually respond. Without serious practice, insight recedes and dims. The texts can then seem meaningless and obscure, or become ritualized cant and doctrinal abstraction (*ti* 體). The philosophical purpose of a sutra is to stimulate and guide a journey. The sutra is a map to be opened up and referenced again and again while traversing what otherwise might be *terra incognita*—the unfamiliar land of one's own mind. As *The Dhammapada* points out:

> No one frees you but yourself.
> No one can, and no one may.
> You yourself must walk the Path:
> Buddhas only show the way.

Time and again, the Master urges his followers not to seek outside their own nature for bodhi. Any external grasping, even at that teaching itself, is pointless because "basically there's not one thing," (*ben lai wu yi wu* 本來無一物). Hence, all teachings can only serve as *upaya* (*fang bian* 方便) or liberative techniques.

Role of the Teacher . . .

The text asks: what is the role of the teacher? In answering, Huineng both challenges and affirms the necessity of relying on a mentor (Skt. *kalyanamitra*; Ch. *shan zhi shi* 善知識).

After passing on the patriarchal robe and bowl to Huineng, the Fifth Patriarch escorted the now Sixth Patriarch to the river to send him off. They boarded a boat, and Hongren took up the oars and began to row. Huineng said,

> "Please, Master, sit down. Your disciple should row."
> The Patriarch replied, "It is appropriate that I take you across."

Huineng said, "When someone is confused, his master takes him across. But when one has awakened, he takes himself across."

Teachers, it would seem, are also a timely expedient. They are necessary, according to Huineng, only if the seeker has become so muddled and alienated from the essential nature that he can no longer see the Way on his own. Losing inner discernment and momentarily straying off course is the only situation in the entire text in which 'seeking outside' is encouraged, even deemed imperative. A Good and Wise mentor outside must be summoned when the inner advisor is weak, unreliable, or unresponsive. The Sixth Patriarch explains,

> If you cannot understand on your own, you must seek out a Good and Wise Advisor who can lead you to see. If you are someone who can awaken on your own, however, do not seek outside. Don't think that I am saying that you can only gain liberation through a Good and Wise Teacher, other than yourself. That is mistaken. Why? Within your own mind there is a good advisor who can awaken you yourself.

As the Sixth Patriarch points out again and again, all of the teachings are merely provisional agents for change. The Dharma can support but never substitute for the necessarily self-determined task of "returning the light to illumine within." One must directly apprehend for oneself, or as the text describes, "see into one's own nature oneself" (*zi jian xing* 自見性). As the above *Dhammapada* verse implies, without self-exertion, even the Buddha cannot save you. Huineng warns his students, "if you let yourself morally stray, become confused, confounded, and all mixed up with wrong thinking, then even if a Good and Wise Advisor gives you instruction, he will not be able to help you."

Dismantling the Familiar . . .

To reinforce this fundamental truth, the Master deconstructs almost all of the then current forms of practice and belief. He also dismantles the exclusive truth claims of various sects or schools of his time—dismantles, but does not destroy them. Rather, he refocuses almost every form of Buddhist belief and devotion through the sharp lens of the essential nature. In doing so, he reveals their expedient purpose and provisional legitimacy, while not denying their utility or demeaning their worth. He points to their pragmatic function (*yong* 用) as liberating techniques, and thereby reaffirms their true purpose, not as fixed dogma but as prescriptive remedies for restoring the 'mind-ground' (*xin di* 心地), fortifying the root nature (*ben xing* 本性).

Hence, when asked about the merit accrued by the famous Buddhist protector Emperor Liang who built temples, supported monks, endowed monasteries, printed sutras, and bestowed charity, Huineng answered, "There truly was no merit and virtue." While charity and generosity create blessings, they in no way constitute merit and virtue. Huineng advises his audience,

> Good and Wise Friends, merit and virtue must manifest from within your own nature; do not seek for them by making donations and offerings. . . . Seeing one's essential nature is merit; equanimity is virtue. To be flexible and unimpeded in thought after thought, always cognizant of the true and wondrous workings of one's original nature—this is called 'merit and virtue.'

What matters most can only be established in the mind and flow from the essential nature.

Thus, Huineng refreshes and refocuses his listeners' view of another form of popular devotion, Pure Land practice. Reciting the

Buddha's name, no matter how loud or long, without a corresponding inner purification, cannot bring liberation. In the Sixth Patriarch's view, seeking rebirth in Amitabha's Western Land of Ultimate Bliss without rectifying one's mind is misguided and fruitless. Huineng informs one of his disciples, Prefect Wei, the Pure Land is as close or far away as a pure mind.

> Good Sir, if the ground-of-the-mind is free of anything unwholesome, the West will not be very far away. If you invoke the Buddha's name yet still hang on to unwholesomeness, it will be hard to gain that rebirth [in the Pure Land].

Rather than viewing the Pure Land as a permanent fixed abode awaiting one's future arrival after death, Huineng sees it as a living, spiritual project in the making. He says, "As the mind is purified, the Buddhaland is purified." The real Pure Land is a pure mind, and must be sought within the nature of human beings, not outside.

> Ordinary deluded people, unaware of their essential nature, do not realize that the Pure Land is within themselves. So, they long to be born in the East, and they long to be born in the West. To the enlightened person all places are the same.

The act of taking Refuge in the Three Treasures (the Buddha, Dharma, and Sangha), which is the formal way of becoming a Buddhist, is also turned inward. "Good and Wise Friends," he urges, "take refuge in and return to the three treasures of your own essential nature." What exactly does that mean? The Sixth Patriarch explains,

> *The Buddha is awakening.*
> *The Dharma is what is right and true.*
> *The Sangha is purity.*

Most people, he laments, "fail to understand this, and so from morning to night they take the Three Refuge Precepts," meaning, they recite this phrase almost like a prayer. He poses this question to his audience: "You say you take refuge with the Buddha, but where is the Buddha? If you do not recognize the Buddha, how can you return to him? Such talk is absurd." Huineng's challenge here is striking: where *exactly* do you imagine the Buddha to be? What do you imagine the Buddha to look like? He is not simply demythologizing the popular otherworldly image of the Buddha that his audience held *in* their minds, but relocating the actual Buddha *to* their own minds. The idol is false; the true Buddha is one's own mind. The Three Jewels and the Three Bodies of the Buddha arise from one's own nature, not from without. They exist right within human nature. He further says,

> If you do not return to the Buddha within, there is nothing you can rely on. Now that you have awakened yourselves, each of you take refuge with the three treasures of your own mind. Inwardly, regulate your mind and character; outwardly, respect others. This is to take refuge with yourself.

Taking refuge with oneself, however, does not mean settling into a self-centered narcissism, or simply trusting one's feelings and unexamined views. Self-nature refuge is a cultivated state of recovering one's true self: one takes refuge in one's own inherent Buddha (awakening), one's own innate Dharma (what is right and true), and one's own intrinsic sangha (inherent purity). "If you cultivate in this way," he says, "this is taking refuge with yourself."

Huineng further maintains that taking refuge is not a one-time act of conversion, but a continuous method of self-correcting and self-affirming—"Constantly use the three treasures of your essential nature to verify and confirm [what is true]." Thus one does not "take refuge" on a given day in a single of ritual devotion, but engages in a uneasing process of returning and relying, in thought-to-thought (*nian nian* 念念). Instead of attaining, there is only maintaining.

Even the *sine qua non* of all Buddhist practice, the moral precepts, are revisited as mind-ground cultivation, rather than seen as a matter of strict observance or propriety. External conformity to a discipline however well-intended, does not guarantee purity or moral integrity. The mind itself has to be precepted, or trued (*zheng* 正), flowing from the nature and aligned with the Way. Formal taking of precepts must be followed by a daily upholding of precepts, until at some point even the idea of upholding vanishes. This state of effortless accord is reminiscent of Confucius's famous passage, "When I was seventy I could yield to the promptings of my own heart (*xin* 心) without transgressing what was right."

At the deepest level of self-cultivation, the precepts hold themselves, from thought-moment to thought-moment. Huineng seems to be saying that one does not simply *take* or even *hold* the precepts, but *becomes* the very spirit of them. According to the text, our natural inclination is towards purity and stillness. If not disturbed by our thoughts or enticed away by our desires, our nature by itself remains pure, still. Thus, Huineng asks,

> *The mind regulated and subdued, why toil following rules?*
> *Your 'steps' straight and true, what use is sitting in meditation?*

Meditation . . .

As the second line of the above verse intimates, even sitting meditation (*zuo chan* 坐禪), seen by many Buddhists as the most direct and ultimate practice, comes in for criticism.

In some ways, some of the text's harshest scrutiny and cautionary injunctions are reserved for meditation. To stop thinking and contemplate stillness is a sickness, not Chan meditation, the Master admonishes. The practice of constant sitting restricts the body and clouds the mind. How, he asks, could it help towards discovering truth? He gives this verse to one disciple who is enamored with the practice of prolonged sitting:

> You can sit without lying down from the moment you're born,
> But when you die, you'll lie down, never again to sit.
> How could you build a solid practice
> On a set of stinking bones?!

This error is dramatically illustrated in Chapter 7, "Lively Encounters." Here a Chan practitioner is introduced who has acquired a big reputation by living in a hut and having devoted himself to constant sitting meditation for twenty years. The Sixth Patriarch's disciple, Xuance, happens to be wandering through the area, and on hearing of Zhihuang's reputation, he pays a visit to his hut. There he asks him, "What are you doing here?"

Thinking he had already realized genuine samadhi, the hermit calmly replies, "Entering concentration."

Xuance says, "You say you are 'entering concentration;' do you have a thought of entering, or are you entering without thought? If you enter without thought, then all insentient things like grass and trees, rocks and stones, should attain 'samadhi.' If you enter with thought, then all sentient beings with consciousness should attain samadhi."

The hermit is speechless. After a while he asks what Xuance's teacher, the Sixth Patriarch, teaches about meditation. Once again, Xuance's answer brings us back to the nature, to the mind-ground teaching. His description of the Sixth Patriarch's teaching on meditation is worth quoting in full:

My teacher explains it as a subtle, wondrous, perfect serenity that interacts both in essence and application with reality as it truly is. Here, the five skandhas are fundamentally empty; the six sensory realms do not exist. One neither enters or comes out of this samadhi concentration, it cannot be settled into or disturbed. The essence of chan concentration is non-dwelling, clinging to nothing; it goes beyond even the act of 'dwelling' in meditative stillness. Chan concentration by its very nature cannot be initiated, and you cannot even conceive the thought or idea of it. The mind is like empty space, yet without even a notion of empty space.

In yet another encounter, when an Imperial envoy dispatched from the palace asks whether it is true, as "the worthy Chan masters of the capital" all teach, that it is absolutely necessary to practice sitting meditation in order to gain an understanding of the Way, the Master retorts,

The Way is realized through the mind. How could it come from sitting? *The Diamond Sutra* says, "If you claim that the Tathagata either sits or lies down, you are traveling a wrong path. Why? Because he neither comes from anywhere, nor goes anywhere." Freedom from birth and death is the Tathagata's pure chan meditation. The still emptiness of all things is the Tathagata's pure chan sitting. Ultimately there is no realization; how much the less 'sitting.'

This answer, as with so many of his exchanges, is not to be taken as absolute Truth, but as a timely and tactical truth aimed at breaking the attachment of the questioner. (This dialogical device, as far as we can ascertain, was the method the Buddha himself employed almost exclusively). The Master undoubtedly would have on another occasion, for another person, insisted that meditation was indispensable. For example, another great Master, Zongmi (780–841), once observed, "While Vimalakirti did say that it was not necessary to sit in meditation, he did not say that it is necessary *not* to sit in meditation." Right here we can see the critical difference between *upaya* as 'skillful means,' and an 'anything-goes' relativism. We also gain an insight into another facet of the direct teaching: total commitment conjoined with total non-attachment, not as alternating moods but in simultaneous equipoise—also known as 'doing-without-doing' (*wu wei* 無為).

The Single-Practice Concentration . . .

Other conventional forms of practice and popular religious activity—memorizing and reciting sutras, erudition, debating, and even "leaving home" to become a monastic—while salutary, and in many ways admirable, will not, according the Master, themselves lead to awakening or wisdom. Used correctly, they liberate; used incorrectly (i.e. with unwholesome intention, either to garner name and fame, or to acquire material or spiritual power), they can actually hinder awakening and deplete virtue. Perfectly legitimate spiritual exercises of the 'great Way' (*da dao* 大道) can all too easily become entangling by-paths, twisted by what Huineng calls a "crooked mind." He cites *The Vimalakirti Sutra* which says, "The direct mind is the place of awakening; the direct mind is the Pure Land."

Thus, he exhorts his students to maintain a pure intention and singleness of purpose, to seek for nothing outside, and to sincerely cultivate one's own mind-ground in every situation; to hold to the 'straight mind' or 'direct mind' whether "walking, standing, sitting, or reclining." He terms this the Single-Practice concentration (*yi xing san mei* 一行三昧), and explains,

> The Single-Practice Samadhi means always maintaining a
> direct mind in all situations. . . . Do not allow the workings
> of your mind to become twisted, while merely talking about
> directness with your mouth; nor expound on the Single-
> Practice Samadhi but fail to cultivate the direct mind. Just
> cultivate with a direct mind and do not cling to anything.

While the overall thrust of the Sixth Patriarch's teaching is *via nega-tiva*, it in no way should be misconstrued as a form of spiritual nihilism or as an encouragement to non-conformist license. The "nothing whatsoever" and "emptiness" the Sixth Patriarch espouses and points his students to is not really empty at all, but wondrous existence itself. Human beings reach their fullest potential, paradoxically, not in striving but in letting go. He says,

> The wondrous nature of people is originally empty; there is
> nothing that can be grasped. And the true emptiness of the
> essential nature is the same.

One is always pure and still yet not clinging to purity or stillness. Or put another way: non-clinging itself *is* purity and stillness. One is naturally, artlessly content and unperturbed, yet not "marked" by a blank, studied indifference or an apathetic withdrawal masquerading as non-attachment. The "true emptiness" described in the text is lively, liberated, responsive, and always appropriate. As this passage describes,

> Those who see their essential nature, can set these up or not
> as they choose. They can come and go freely, unhindered
> and spontaneous. Everything they do and all their words are
> appropriate, timely, and according to need. Wherever and
> however they appear, they never depart from the inherent

nature. They are just "realizing the spiritual powers of self-mastery" and "the samadhi of playfulness." This is called "seeing the nature."

The emptiness Huineng describes is more of an unrestricted liberation born of a profound insight into the nature of reality, and the freedom of action that understanding confers. As in the uninterrupted "great Samadhi" the Master refers to in which there is no entering or leaving it, so too within the 'wondrous existence of true emptiness' the essential nature does not vacillate or falter. It is not subject to mood swings, ups and downs, or dependent on shifting conditions.

> It does not arrive or leave; and has no location: neither inside nor outside nor in the middle. Unborn, undying, its essence and appearance is 'just so; as it really is.' It is permanent and unchanging—it is called 'the Way.'

Two additional themes should be addressed, as they are generally what most readers would expect to be the central subjects of *The Platform Sutra*: meditation and enlightenment.

More On Meditation . . .

Anyone looking for a meditation manual in this sutra will be disappointed. *The Platform Sutra* gives no precise method of practice, nor does it spell out in any detail how to meditate. Only one chapter, and the shortest one at that, is specifically devoted to meditation. Whereas, a chapter five times longer, Chapter Six "Repent and Renew," is given over to the preparation for meditation: cleansing the heart and straightening the mind. Meditation (*zuo chan* 坐禪), according to the text, simply consists of not losing sight of our natural purity or disturbing our intrinsic equanimity.

> You might say it [sitting meditation] is fixating on purity, yet people's nature is basically pure. Only because of confused thinking is its natural true "thus-being" obscured. Only put an end to your confused thinking, and the nature is pure of itself. . . . Good and Wise Friends, what does "sitting meditation" mean? To engage in this practice means you remain unhindered and unobstructed. Your mind and thoughts do not stir no matter what good and bad state or external situation presents itself. That is called "sitting." And to inwardly discern the unmoving stability of the essential nature—this is called "meditation."

In other words, our original nature, our fundamental mind, is in itself prajna samadhi. Concentration (*ding* 定) is inseparable from wisdom (Skt. *prajna;* Ch. *hui* 慧), and wisdom is not something meditation can bring about or build up, as it is fundamentally possessed by everyone from the outset and all along. This innate completeness is referred to in the text as "thus-being," (*ru shi* 如是), or alternately as our "true ultimate nature" (*zhen ru ben xing* 真如本性).

In examining the text closely one would be almost forced to conclude that for Huineng meditation is nothing special. In fact, the hype and misconceptions surrounding sitting meditation then, as perhaps now, could make it a potential liability rather than a spiritual asset. Meditation does not necessarily end confusion; more often meditation exposes it. Or, if diligently taken up, it might momentarily dislocate our confusion. It too is *upaya*—an expedient tool that allows us to interrupt the habitual stream of attachments and distractions that leads us away from the ever-present wondrous functioning of our true mind. The ultimate goal is not to stop thinking altogether, but simply to "stop the mad mind" from dominating consciousness. For, "when the mad mind stops," as *The Surangama Sutra* reminds us, "that very stopping *is* bodhi." The meditation Huineng advances is simply clarity of mind in every situation, or 'stillness-in-movement.' He says,

> Good and Wise Friends, what does "sitting meditation" mean? To engage in this practice means you remain unhindered and unobstructed. Your mind and thoughts do not stir no matter what good and bad state or external situation presents itself. That is called "sitting." And to inwardly discern the unmoving stability of the essential nature—this is called "meditation."

The expression preferred by the Sixth Patriarch is 'seeing the nature' (*jian xing* 見性) as opposed to "getting enlightened." Chan or zen does not consist of entering a trance-like absorption, or in working oneself into a state of transcendental bliss, but in simply putting an end to confused thinking and frantic grasping.

The dhyana meditation the Sixth Patriarch teaches is a complete way of living, and requires a total reorientation of one's mind. It is not just sitting on a cushion with an empty mind, but a mental-emotional state of equanimity carried on 24/7, while walking, standing, sitting, and even in sleep. As mentioned above, it is called "single-practice samadhi," (*yi xing san mei* 一行三昧), and describes a constant and alert presence of mind, body, and emotions *in action*, rather than a disconnected, reclusive *inaction*. The Sixth Patriarch's meditation consists of an uninterrupted mindfulness in which there is no attachment to anything, not even meditation itself. He instructs his students,

> Simply let your mind be like empty space, without attaching to an idea of your mind as empty space; responding appropriately without any hindrance, clear of mind whether moving or still. Distinctions like 'worldly' and 'holy', forgotten;

subject and object, dissolved. Essence and appearance are
'just so; as they really are'—then there is no time you are not
in chan concentration.

Thus, when the Sixth Patriarch refers to the "place of awakening" (Skt. *bodhimanda*; Ch. *pu ti dao chang* 菩提道場) it is not to be taken literally as referring to a special location, or even to a specific practice, like sitting meditation, but to a clear state of mind. Moreover, he asserts that the direct mind itself is the monastery. The text states,

> Good and Wise Friends, if you wish to cultivate [this practice]
> you can do it at home—you do not have to be in a monastery.
> If you can cultivate at home you are like the person of the
> East whose mind is good; conversely, being in a monastery
> but not cultivating is like the person of the West whose mind
> harbors evil. Just purify your mind; that is the 'West' of your
> essential nature.

Cultivating the mind turns anyplace into sacred space; conversely, without actual cultivation, even the monastery becomes profane. The distant Western Pure Land of Amitabha is not distant at all; it is just the here-and-now pure mind.

The contemplative stance expounded in the text is not even presented as a "practice." In fact, one would be hard-pressed to condense *The Platform Sutra's* contemplative teachings into a booklet on "how to sit," or to recast it into the genre of currently popular manuals with titles like "a practical guide to meditation." The closest Huineng comes to actual instruction on meditation is this:

> The practice of sitting meditation basically consists of not
> fixating on the mind, nor on purity, nor is it just sitting

motionless. If you speak of "fixing on the mind," this mind is fundamentally false. You should realize that the mind is like an illusion, with nothing at all to grab onto.

Notions such as 'establishing a practice' or 'setting up a meditation routine' simply do not appear in the text. Huineng instead describes a "Samadhi of playfulness," which is just another expression for "seeing the nature." He explains,

When your essential nature is free from error, unobstructed, undisturbed and unconfused, when prajna oversees and illuminates your every thought, and you are far removed from the superficial appearances of things, independent and free absolutely everywhere and anywhere—what is there to "set up?"

Chan (abbr. of *channa* 禪那, from Sanskrit *dhyana*), is not taken up at a monastic retreat, nor is it then put aside upon returning home. Sitting at Huineng's feet, one would never ask, "How can I keep up my meditation state after the retreat?"

The Sixth Patriarch would consider it the height of folly to hanker for altered states of consciousness, or even to imagine and visualize pure abodes. His dhyana dwells nowhere, yet manifests in and through all the activities of daily life. One need not withdraw from the world, for as he reminds his students, the true mind makes the monastery, not the other way around. The mind made straight, or 'trued,' needs nothing. Such intrinsic completeness he calls 'empty' (*kong* 空) and 'not dwelling' (*wu zhu* 無住) indicating not the absence of something, but the total sufficiency of our true nature.

Wherever possible therefore, we have translated non-attachment and non-dwelling into their positive equivalents. As in this central passage:

1

> Good and Wise Friends, this teaching of ours from its very
> inception has taken freedom from thought as its source,
> freedom from appearances as its essence, and freedom from
> clinging as its basis. "Freedom from appearances" means
> to be detached from appearances while in the midst of
> appearances. "Freedom from thought" means detachment
> from thought in the midst of thought. And, "freedom from
> clinging" Is the basic nature of human beings. . . . Our true
> nature is eternally free and independent.

Unobstructed freedom-in-virtue is the hallmark of a cultivator
of the Way. This person abides in what the Master calls the "great
Samadhi" (*da san mei* 大三昧), a cultivated state of unimpeded
awareness in which one is constantly responding, constantly still.
Genuine samadhi, as the Sixth Patriarch insists, does not dwell in
emptiness or cling to stillness. It is not even entered, because it *is* in
itself the fundamental ground of our being, the very essence of our
full human capacity.

On Enlightenment . . .

There exists a great deal of confusion, both then and now, about 'enlightenment' (*wu* 悟; *kai wu* 開悟). Many of the Master's disciples
sought it fervently, almost obsessively. As this text makes clear, however, enlightenment is not something one gets, but rather something
one becomes, or changes into. Even speaking of an "enlightenment
experience" is too facile. One, because an 'experience' suggests a
passing event or momentary feeling. And two, it implies an 'experi-
encer' who stands apart from and receives or has the experience. The
"I" who has an "experience" are two, not one. Thus, the term 'awakening' more appropriately conveys the idea that *wu* 悟 is a deepening

inner awareness, a transformative understanding. It signifies a radical revision of the "me," to the extent that the person who realizes it is not the same person who set out in search of it.

Most importantly, enlightenment cannot be transferred or transmitted from one person to another. For example, when queried by the monk Yinzong about what Dharma the Fifth Patriarch transmitted to him, he simply answers, "There was no transfer. We merely discussed seeing the nature. There was no discussion of dhyana Samadhi or liberation." In other words, they simply talked about what was self-evident to one who "sees the nature." The Dharma is realized and embodied, not transmitted. When pressed by his own students about who would receive the Patriarchal "transmission," Huineng simply replies, "Whoever realizes the Way has it; those with an unattached mind get it."

Nor is awakening 'sudden' as *dun* (頓) has been widely translated into English, conveying an image of a cathartic moment of enlightenment, and the expectation of an abrupt, out-of-the-blue thunderous flash of perfect insight. Rather *dun* means non-dual and direct. It describes not a *kind* of enlightenment, but an *approach* to self-cultivation that is straightforward, not interposed by stages or provisional expedients. It is immediate only in the strict sense of the word—*im*-mediate (lit. 'not mediated'). It is not mediated through any other process, such as thinking, deliberating, willing, or reasoning. This direct, non-discursive approach to understanding is succinctly conveyed in the passage cited above: "this teaching of ours from its very inception has taken freedom from thought as its source, freedom from appearances as its essence, and freedom from clinging as its basis" (*wu nian, wu xiang, wu zhu wei ben* 無念無相無住為本).

It is entirely possible that the "direct" teaching might take longer in time to master than the "gradual" teaching. It does not, after all, describe an experience *per se*, but a disposition and commitment to a particular and, we should add, demanding approach to practice. Also, as the Sixth Patriarch is quick to point out, even the labels "direct" and "gradual" are merely provisional terms for the Buddha's single source-teaching that holds to neither and sets up nothing.

> The Master said to the assembly, "The Dharma is originally a single school; it is people who think 'north' and 'south'. The Dharma is of one kind; but the understanding of it may be 'direct' or 'gradual'. Dharma itself is neither 'direct' nor 'gradual'. Rather it is people who are sharp or dull. Hence the terms 'direct' and 'gradual.'"

Nonetheless, he points out, people have differing capacities, differing needs. So, the single direct teaching, like the staged indirect teaching, is both expediently shaped and formulated to accommodate these differences.

> Good and Wise Friends, the correct teaching is basically neither "direct" nor "gradual"; it is people's dispositions that are sharp or dull. The deluded person who cultivates gradually, and the more aware person who [cultivates] directly, converge: each recognizes their original mind, each sees their original nature. In this, they are the same. Therefore, "direct" and "gradual" are just provisional terms.

Readers inclined to see Buddhist writings as abstruse metaphysical treatises will find *The Platform Sutra* refreshingly artless and spare. Those expecting a sutra to delve into the supernatural and other-worldly will be surprised at how down-to-earth and here-and-now this text is. *The Platform Sutra* is humanistic to its core. As Huineng says in a verse,

The Buddha Dharma is right here in the world,
There is no awakening apart from this world.

The Platform Sutra speaks to the human condition, to the things that are both timely and timeless: fleeting existence, dissatisfaction, longing, and the emptiness of material things, as well as happiness, life's deepest meaning, liberation, wonder, and our capacity for profound wisdom. Though a product of the Tang dynasty (618–906 C.E.), its style is surprisingly modern; its language clear and accessible. It is perhaps within one cover, the best introduction to the Buddha's teachings and the most advanced index to its practice. Our teacher, Master Hsüan Hua, once said, "*The Platform Sutra* is all you need to study and understand to be a Buddhist; to become a Buddha."

SCHOLARSHIP NOTES AND ISSUES

Huineng (638–713) was the Sixth Patriarch in China, and the thirty-third in Patriarchal descendents from the time of the Buddha in India. He was the immediate successor of Master Hongren (601–674). The Sixth Patriarch himself wrote nothing, nor left any record of his life or teaching. This text, *The Sixth Patriarch's Dharma Jewel Platform Sutra* (六祖法寶壇經 *liu zu fa bao tan jing*) represents the only account we have of his life and lectures. So highly regarded is his place in the Buddhist tradition, that to our knowledge this text is the only one that has been accorded the title "sutra," a term traditionally reserved only for teachings directly attributed to the Buddha.

Two versions of *The Sixth Patriarch's Sutra* are most widely available today: the Zongbao text, and an earlier and briefer surviving manuscript called the "Dunhuang text." The Dunhuang manuscript, the earliest extant rendition of the Platform Sutra, was probably written around 780 C.E. Its title "Dunhuang" refers to the place it was uncovered. This occurred during the excavations of a sealed cave in the early 1900s near the oasis town of Dunhuang in the northwestern area of China along the famed Silk Road. It may have itself been a copy of an earlier version(s) now unavailable to us. The Zongbao version, the text translated here, dates from the Yuan dynasty (1271–1368), and was assembled in 1291. The Zongbao is a more mature version of the Dunhuang text, being longer by close to 10,000 characters. This version has come to be known as the Zongbao text in reference to the Chinese monk by that name who did the compilation in 1291. The Zongbao text (Taisho Vol. 48; Number 2008) was incorporated into the Ming tripitaka and remains the most popular and widely used edition to date.

Zongbao himself wrote a postface regarding the origin of the compilation and editing of *The Platform Sutra*. He noted, "I saw three different copies [of *The Platform Sutra*], all had their pros and cons, and the printing plates were gone. Therefore, I compared and edited the text; corrected the errors and elaborated the abridgments. I also added 'the encounters and questions of disciples,' so that learners can get the complete essence of Caoxi." This particular version also includes a prefatory introduction attributed to Fahai of the Tang Dynasty. Titled "General Introduction" (略序), it appears as the first section of this new translation. It was this version that Master Hsüan Hua lectured on at Gold Mountain Monastery in San Francisco in the late 1960s. In other arrangements, Fahai's preface is inserted into the Appendix at the end of the Sutra, and entitled "Attachment—the record of conditions for the 6th Patriarch" (六祖大師緣記外記).

Scholars have struggled for decades to reconstruct the history of *The Platform Sutra* in its various forms over time, to little avail. We may never know with certainty who wrote the text, or when it was compiled, or what the earliest version(s) may have looked like.

The complexity of such a task is freighted with lacunae in time and records, not to mention erasure by just the raw elements of nature, and even hostile human action. Burning libraries, smashing icons, and overwriting manuscripts are after all, not new to human history. Nor is the discovery of ancient texts previously unknown to the world.

The conjectured "earlier" versions upon which later extant copies are presumably based, will in all likelihood never be found. The "original" teachings recorded by hand, and passed along from disciple to disciple were undoubtedly subject to scribal errors, lapses in memory, and emendations over time. It is equally probable that the texts were reorganized, adjusted, clarified, and either expanded or contracted from compiler to compiler. It would be important here to point out that in the Buddhist tradition such activity is quite normal and not in itself problematic. Authorship is not necessarily the same as "authoritative," nor is historical precession the *sine qua non* measure of authenticity.

In Western academic discourse, on the other hand, discussion of such issues gets channeled into a peculiar paradigmatic chute called "religious studies" or "comparative religion." Originally known as *religionwissenschaft* (lit. 'science of religion'), it is a product of nineteenth-century European concerns about the historical and scientific basis of religion, and particularly about the Western colonial encounter with the "other," largely Hindu, Islamic, and Buddhist teachings. This social science framing is a relatively new and very specialized way of thinking about "religion," and despite its claim of universal objectivity, might be a culture-bound product of a special historical experience. It may or may not hold enduring relevance for other traditions and experience. Most methodologies, as Hans-Georg

Gadamer pointed out, too often pre-structure interpretation, since the method one uses determines what one will find.

Contemporary scholars are now beginning to ask if the assumptions, methods, theories, and conceptions of knowledge derived from Western science and its social sciences might not actually reduce and distort what they claim to investigate and explain. Even early researchers doubted that they truly held the keys to understanding Buddhism. But recently the discussion is turning to more basic questions: are the logic, norms, and procedures of the Western social sciences as they have evolved over the centuries in the West, universally applicable and their findings universally valid? More to the point, are their questions the ones we should be concerned with in reading this sutra?

The late M. G. S. Hodgson, eminent historian of Islam at the University of Chicago, observed that Buddhism was framed through a particular Eurocentric lens that skewed our understanding of it. A particular bias of Western thinking led us to define these teachings as an 'ism,' created by Gautama himself. This framing presupposed three things: one, that the Buddha was a systematic philosopher; two, that the first form of this cumulative tradition is best and the most genuine; and, three, that 'religion' is a doctrine, a system of which all else is the logical consequence. Hodgson noted that none of this is true of Buddhism.

Instead, the Buddhist phenomenon was much more a cumulative tradition with a different sort of validity. The Buddha's teachings occurred as an "event," a sequence of dialectic responses pragmatically concerned with ending human suffering by liberating the mind from attachments. Hodgson concluded, "That we accept the fact that this is not (and, as an expression of the Buddhists' ultimate concern, could not be) a philosophical conception about which we may calmly converse in sovereign detachment will indicate that we are at the gateway to an understanding of it."[3]

Hodgson's observations seem to be borne out by a close reading of the Buddhist texts themselves. For example, Huineng makes the nearly identical point about the Dharma not being an 'ism' created by Gautama when he asserts, "This teaching has been passed down from sages of the past; it is not my own wisdom." And again, when tracing the source of the Dharma to the Buddhas of antiquity, he describes a teaching without beginning or end. He says, "Since the past, numberless Buddhas have responded to the needs of the world—too many to be counted." The Sixth Patriarch's statements thus suggest another standard for authority, one not tied to a single historical founder, or even to a single definitive scripture. In Huineng's simple statement lies a fundamentally different approach to knowing religiously.

Rather than locating authority in a creed or adherence to accepted dogmas of faith and belief (ortho-doxy), the Patriarch locates it in a fluid, living teaching. Authenticity is conferred through direct experience and confirmed under the guidance of a wise mentor. In the Buddhist tradition, authority is largely diachronic, that is to say, it flows through time, continuously reestablishing itself in and through changing conditions. Authority is not synchronic, set down at one particular time, past or present, and thus fixed in stone. In this more orthopraxic orientation, in which much of South and East Asian philosophical and spiritual 'teachings' (not 'isms') locate themselves, truth is measured not so much in rightness of thought, or allegiance to a Book, or its author, but to a 'Way' deemed conducive to wisdom

---

3 Hodgson's remarks, along with a fuller treatment of these issues can be found in Guy Richard Welbon, *The Buddhist Nirvana and Its Western Interpreters,* Chicago: University of Chicago Press (1968).

and the embodiment of virtue. As Julia Ching, the noted scholar of East Asian religions put it,

> The debate in China has always been over a right way of living, that is, about the correctness of ideas regarding the good life. The issue is thus not so much one of the correctness of certain intellectual propositions, than of wisdom, which concerns insights into the whole of life, of man and his place in the universe, the knowledge of which must be accompanied by virtuous behavior.[4]

Here it is less important to know "who" said it, than to inquire into the appropriateness of "what" was said. And even what is said needs further inspection, motivated by a concern for *how* it is manifested, lived, and embodied. The use of the term "Way" does not indicate a fuzziness or imprecision with thought, but rather an entirely different way of thinking.

To illustrate, the Buddhist texts construct a four-fold scaffolding for determining the validity of any text purporting to be "Dharma." Known as *The Catuhpratisaranasutra* ("Sutra of the Four Refuges"), it establishes a precise method for interpretation using a sequentially staged process of ascending 'reliances': 1) relying on the teaching (Skt. *dharma*) over the person (Skt. *purusa*); 2) the spirit (Skt. *artha*) over the letter (Skt. *vyanjana*); 3) the precise meaning (Skt. *nitartha*) over the provisional (Skt. *neyartha*); and, 4) direct knowledge (Skt. *jnana*) over discursive knowledge (Skt. *vijnana*).

The Buddha himself encouraged his listeners to "know for themselves" rather than to merely rely on tradition, the authority of the texts, or even a personal devotion to the teacher with the idea that

---

4 Julia Ching, *To Acquire Wisdom: The Way of Wang Yang-ming.* New York: Columbia University Press, (1976).

"this is our teacher." Thus the single and indispensable instrument for determining authenticity of a text is direct insight (*prajna*), which would imply that authority must ultimately reside in a personal replication of the Buddha's awakening experience. In other words, theory must be tested and confirmed by practice.

Neither the Buddha nor the Sixth Patriarch wrote anything. So can we know with certainty what the Buddha said? Or, what the Sixth Patriarch said? Historically speaking, the answer may be "no." Nonetheless we do have ways of determining whether what they are purported to have said is valid, reliable, and accords with the Dharma. How do we decide what is the teaching, the *word* (Skt. *buddhavacana*) of the Buddha? The Buddha himself gave this reply: "Whatever is conducive to liberation and not bondage—that is my teaching."

> Of whatever teachings (dhamma), O Gotami, you can assure yourself: "These teachings lead to dispassion (viraga), not to passion (saraga); to freedom from bondage (visamyoga), not to bondage (samgoya); to decrease [in possessions], not to increase; to few desires, not to many; to contentment, not to discontent; to solitude, not to socializing; to energy, not to indolence; to ease in maintaining oneself, not to difficulty—indeed you may consider 'this is the Dhamma, this is the vinaya, this is the teaching of the Teacher (sasthusasana).'"
> —*Cullavaga*, X, 4

Clearly, the Dharma as the "word" of the Buddha, is not a closed canon, either in time or place.

Taken together, we have from within the Buddhist tradition itself, criteria for evaluating anything that purports to be the Dharma, as well as explicit guidelines for establishing authenticity. Using criteria derived from Buddhist sources themselves we are presented with an alternative frame of reference to the social science based approach, along with an entirely different set of markers by which to determine, "Is this the word of the Buddha?" To undertake such a task may be as daunting and elusive as the narrowly historicist approach, but is it any less worthwhile or promising?

In all translation the question of context arises: where does this text belong? Where do we locate it? Is it Chinese, or more precisely medieval Chinese? Is it a "Chan" text, or "early Chan" text? Purely Chinese, or sinicized Indian Buddhism? Does it represent the actual words of Huineng, or his followers, or is it purely a product of factionalist rival schools vying for institutional identity or supremacy, as some would argue? What is fact? What is legend? An earlier translator, Philip Yampolsky, wrestled with these questions in trying to ascertain what was probable, improbable, credible, unlikely, certain, provable, untenable and so on, in regards to this text. He came to the conclusion that we might never know, and therefore should suspend judgment until more evidence becomes available—if it ever does.

Such ambiguities inhere not only to Buddhist sutras. Similar doubts and questions could be, and have been raised about other major works both East and West, including the Bible, the Koran, the Iliad and Odyssey, and the Daodejing, as well as the works of Aesop, Confucius, and even Shakespeare.

To the modern reader, most of these issues may be of little concern or interest. These great works continue to be translated and widely read. We read them for reasons that reason alone may not fully explain. Why? Perhaps because questions of their origins, authenticity, and authorship notwithstanding, they continue to speak to us directly about what it means to be human, and stimulate us to wonder and worry about the world, our place in it, where we come from and what lies beyond the grave. Of more immediate, and perhaps more lasting interest then is what *The Platform Sutra* itself asks us to concern ourselves with. What does it say? What does it mean? What is it asking us to consider and to do? Each reader will need to answer this for him- or herself. The Sixth Patriarch himself, as will become clear in reading this text, would not expect anyone, then or now, to do anything more or less. And it is this direct approach, both in letter and spirit that best describes the purport of the Sixth Patriarch Sutra.

ON TRANSLATION

Due to the existential nature of the text, we have attempted wherever possible to translate most of the Sutra's key terms and passages into realistic, psychodynamic language. We have also tried to avoid lapsing into dualistic expressions, so ubiquitous in English idiom and usage that we hardly detect them and the underlying worldview they represent.

Language itself interprets and gives meaning more than it simply translates words. Early English translations of Buddhist texts are thus understandably freighted with Judeo-Christian concepts, connotations, and semantics. The English language is not a neutral filter through which Huineng's teachings enter into our understanding. Rather, it is more like a prism that invariably colors and refracts what it seeks to convey. For example, many Western phrasings reflect ideas and attitudes rooted in a dualistic worldview: right/wrong, good/bad, deviant/proper, heresy/orthodoxy, true/false, sacred/secular, Creator/creation, and this world/other world. Moreover, there is a strong almost Manichean dichotomy presumed between the divine/human, worldly/transcendent, mind/body, and matter/spirit.

One finds as well a notable tendency, especially in religious expression, toward judgmental pronouncements, teleological causation, and beginning/end bracketing. Even the words/concept "religion" and

"Buddhism" are a poor fit for what might be better termed 'teaching' or 'path.'

All of this often results in confusion and unintentional misinterpretations. If English translations of classical Chinese are too facilely rendered we end up thinking Buddhist concepts are closely akin to our own familiar categories of thought and feeling, which they often are not. On the other hand, if the translation is awash with language too foreign and unfamiliar to us, the text becomes exotic and indecipherable, which it is not. For example, key concepts like the Sixth Patriarch's non-dualism can come across as mystical gibberish, and his non-attachment as a life-denying Oriental nihilism or antinomian anything-goes relativism. They are none of these; but poor translation makes them so.

In this new translation we have consciously struggled to avoid these tendencies, and as much as possible to find English expression that is clear, faithful to the original, and as free as possible from some of the most egregious semantic pitfalls of the target language. We have attempted to use language that was *in* the culture but not too much *of* the culture.

Thus a common translation such as "cutting off afflictions" (*fan nao duan* 煩惱斷) is retranslated here as "changing afflictions" to convey the idea of interchangeability between the afflictions and awakening; for to 'sever' the afflictions would be to sever the potential for bodhi. 'Change,' as well accents the key psychological direction of self-cultivation: transformation and restoration. Moreover, bodhi (*puti* 菩提) is translated as "awakening" rather than "enlightenment" to convey its meaning as a continuous process, rather than static attainment; something enacted in thought-after-thought, from situation to situation, requiring alertness, flexibility, and active discernment. As in,

> Good and Wise Friends, ordinary people are themselves
> Buddhas, and affliction itself is awakening. In one past
> moment of confused thought you are just an ordinary person.
> If the very next thought is awakened, you are a Buddha.
> Previous thoughts clinging to sensory states are afflictions;
> and succeeding thoughts unattached to states is bodhi.

The sutra throughout seems to deliberately avoid any sense of finality, of beginning and end, or other mutually exclusive split-pairings such as between mind and body, self and other, Buddha and living beings, this world and other worlds. Most importantly, although the text obviously touches on the profoundly spiritual, it does so by never departing from the essentially human.

> The myriad dharmas, absolutely everything, are within the
> nature of all people.

For the awakened, the Sixth Patriarch tells us, the nature of reality is one continuous and unbroken whole, and the entire Dharmarealm is not beyond one's own mind or outside of one's own nature.

If the translation still reveals any of the regrettable tendencies noted above, or fails to convey the immediacy, energy, and wonder of this work, the fault is ours not the text's.

ON INTERPRETATION

The fish trap exists because of the fish. Once you've gotten the fish you can forget the trap. The rabbit snare exists because of the rabbit. Once you've gotten the rabbit, you can forget the snare. Words exist because of meaning. Once you've gotten the meaning, you can forget the words. Where can I find a man who has forgotten words so I can talk with him? —Chuangzi

In language it is simply required that it convey the meaning.

—Analects of Confucius

In working with a classical text of this nature, our ability to get at the meaning is handicapped if we ask only, "What is the author(s) trying to *say?*" or "What do the words mean?" This can easily turn into a pedantic exercise of dictionary searching for equivalents in the target language, assuming they can be found. Moreover, an overly literal rendering that nails down the letter can stifle or even lose the spirit of the text. Here, we achieve a superb focus but the field has become irrelevant.

But if we also ask "What is it/he trying to *do?*" and "What are we being led to *feel?*" we enlarge the scope of the inquiry, and broaden the contextual field to include the emotive and existential thrust of the text. Here we are not just reading the text, but reading ourselves as we are challenged and changed through a serious engagement with the text.

To this end, we have found extremely helpful the following:

First, the brilliant work of the French classicist, Pierre Hadot.[5] His insights into early Western philosophical texts provide a useful lens through which to view *The Platform Sutra* of the Sixth Patriarch. Hadot argues that ancient philosophers aimed less at imparting systems of thought and ready-made knowledge than at cultivating an enlightened way of living, and in providing training that would foster their students' efforts to carry this out. The texts themselves were "therapeutic"—*intended, in the first instance, to form people and*

5 Pierre Hadot, (1922–2010) was a French philosopher and historian of philoso-phy specializing in ancient texts. All quotes taken from P. Hadot *Philosophy as a Way of Life,* Oxford, Blackwell (1995); and, *What Is Ancient Philosophy?* Harvard Univer-sity Press (2002),

to transform souls. The transmission of a purely abstract knowledge was not the teachers' goal. Their instructions were pragmatic: to be applied, lived directly, and embodied. The 'doing' of philosophy entailed study and practicing a method of spiritual exercises in learning to live the philosophical life. Hadot writes,

> Ancient philosophy presented itself as a 'therapeutics' and that this goal meant *doing* philosophy. In this study/practice more than theses, one teaches ways, methods, and spiritual exercises; dogmas have only a secondary aspect.

The exercises were "spiritual" because they required effort, training, and a serious purpose of will to correct entrenched habits and effect a reorientation in one's whole way of being. The aim of the teacher and the text (which was seen as a direct or indirect echo of the oral instructions of the teacher) was not to transmit knowledge, but to produce a certain psychic effect in the reader or listener. The encounter was intended more to form than to inform. The texts born of this tradition came embedded with spiritual exercises aimed at realizing a transformation of one's vision of the world and a metamorphosis of one's personality.

So too, we would argue, is the aim of *The Platform Sutra.* When a student asks the Master which of the "vehicles" (schools or traditions of Buddhism) is the correct one given that they all differ and seem to contradict each other, he answers:

> Vehicles are methods of practice; not subjects for debate. Cultivate yourself; don't ask me. At all times, your own essential nature is itself "truly as it is."

This sutra is clearly "philosophical" in Hadot's sense. It aims at producing an effect upon and an affect *in* the reader. The Master is trying to get his disciples, and by extension the reader, to stop and consider, to act, feel, and live in a certain way. The Sixth Patriarch is not trying to indoctrinate, nor even set up a school of thought. His aim, to borrow Hadot's phrase, is "therapeutic." Huineng stirs his students from their complacency, and purposely unsettles them. He stimulates them to inquire, to take up a practice, and to directly engage their own minds, rather than to believe in a doctrinal exposition, however cogent and credible.

Huineng himself avoids calling his method a system of thought, or even a Teaching. He says, "If I said I had a teaching to give others, I would be deceiving you. Depending on the situation, I merely use expedients to untie people's bonds, and provisionally call it 'samadhi.'" His goal it seems is not to be worshipped as an enlightened teacher, but to set his students on a course of self-cultivation leading them to directly awaken on their own. Put another way, he asks his students "to walk the same path the Buddha(s) walk." Anything else is provisional, expedient, secondary. He deflects attention from himself the teacher, even as he is about to die, and instead redirects his students to the teaching. He tells them,

> After I pass away, don't indulge in worldly sentiment. If you cry tears like rain, receive condolences, or wear mourning garments, you are no longer my disciples; all of this runs counter to the Teaching. Just recognize your original mind and see your fundamental nature.

By rephrasing our question from "What was the Sixth Patriarch trying to say?" to, "What was the Sixth Patriarch attempting to do?" we are able in some degree to enter into the dynamic dialogues from which the text emerged. We engage the material more intimately, as if sitting as participant-observers in the Sixth Patriarch's presence, and push ourselves to reach beyond the words to get the meaning, as in the Zhuangzi quote above. Otherwise, we are left just holding the empty snare.

The "therapeutic" thrust of the text could explain why many scholars experience frustration in attempting to systematize the Sixth Patriarch's "doctrine," or ascertain which specific teaching method he used. *The Platform Sutra* is a record of his teachings under particular conditions while facing specific situations. As such, it is purposively less a philosophical argument for establishing truth, than a compass for taking readings and finding one's way. It resembles a manual intended to guide hands-on application; a suggestive field guide for exploring one's own mind and seeing one's own true nature, not in a remove from the world, but right within the often all-too-real immediate and shifting conditions of the world.

If anything the text is meant as a corrective to dogmatism and counterweight to a blind, faith-based religious persuasion. It proffers a series of accessible, pragmatic lessons for self-cultivation. And like the Buddha in *The Kalama-sutta,* Huineng exhorts the audience members to "know directly for themselves," instead of simply relying on conventional authority. The Master leaves it up to his disciples to take it up or not, only claiming that, "If you fail to cultivate in this way, you will just be an ordinary person. But the moment you put it into practice, you yourself are equal to the Buddhas." In short, as with almost all of the Buddhist teachings, the decision to accept or reject them is left entirely up to the individual. In his closing words to the large gathering assembled at Dafan Temple to formally receive his teaching, the Master says,

> If you can see your nature right while these words are
> uttered, then even if we are a thousand miles apart, you will

be always at my side. If you do not awaken to these words, then face-to-face, we are a thousand miles apart—so why did you bother coming so far to see me?! Take care; go well.

Second, we used the "concept cluster" approach to identify core concepts and make sense of the text's overall thrust. For this we are indebted to the innovative work of Henry Rosemont and Roger Ames in translating and interpreting classical Chinese sources. They write, "the idea of concept-clusters is a great aid to translating and understanding texts written against conceptual backgrounds that differ from our own, and can provide a means of giving the 'other' their otherness without making them either *wholly* other, or, equally mischievous, more simple-minded versions of ourselves."[6] This technique looks for a centering concept, for instance, *ethics* or *virtue* or *justice*, around which many of the other ideas/terms cohere. Rather than trying to translate and interpret each term in isolation, we try to see them in relation to other terms in the cluster. A 'gathering' of sorts begins to emerge where once separate characters or concepts now integrate into a 'cluster' of related and overlapping meanings.

If we view *The Platform Sutra* through the lens of "concept clusters" we see a distinct pattern emerge: nothing. The text is rife with recurring phrasings and concepts expressing the negative: 'not,' 'without,' 'not having,' 'free from,' 'absence of,' 'nothing,' 'empty,' 'apart from,' 'markless,' 'formless,' and so on. This, on its face, might seem to indicate uncertainty, imprecision, vagueness, or even worse, a perverse nihilism or extreme relativism. In fact, the negative concept-clustering is purposeful and telling. It makes perfect sense when viewed from

6 Henry Rosemont Jr. and Roger T. Ames, "On Translation & Interpretation." in *Eastwards: Western Views on East Asian Culture,* edited by Frank Kraushaar. Bern: Peter Lang (2010).

the text's fundamental ground: the inherent wholeness, sufficiency, purity, and non-duality of the essential nature. If true, there is nothing to do, nothing to get. Nothing, paradoxically, is everything.

Upon hearing the line from *The Vajra Sutra*, "*Let your mind be unattached, clinging to nothing,*" Huineng proclaims to his own teacher:

> *How unexpected! The essential nature is intrinsically pure.*
>
> *How unexpected! The essential nature is originally unborn and undying.*
>
> *How unexpected! The essential nature is complete in itself, lacking nothing.*
>
> *How unexpected! The essential nature is fundamentally still and unmoving.*
>
> *How unexpected! From the essential nature the myriad dharmas come to be.*

Note, as well, his counter-verse to Shenxiu, where he asserts, "basically there's not one thing/where could dust alight?"

Since the original nature is whole and complete in itself, lacking nothing, the activity of looking elsewhere and longing for more only confound it. The exhortation "go back to the root; return to the source," suggests movement, but in an almost counter-intuitive direction. Advancing in the Way is a return, the optimal speed is stillness, the greatest strength, letting go. By letting go of the unnecessary, jettisoning the extraneous, we recover the natural fullness of our being, paradoxically called "true emptiness," and "grasping for nothing." As the Daodejing puts it, "in the Tao, the only motion is returning; the only useful quality, weakness (loose grip)." This is also called "learning by subtraction," and resonates with another idea of the quietist persuasion, "effortlessness" (*wu wei* 無為, lit. 'without doing' or 'non-action').

The Sixth Patriarch always teaches *from* and *to* the essential nature (*zi xing, ben xing* 自性; 本性). This is why he can, perhaps *must*, describe the core teaching of his 'school' as no teaching whatsoever. To establish any teaching or 'ism' would imply that the essential nature was lacking, deficient, in need of repair or even redemption. The ideas of "no thought, no mark, no attaching," when viewed from within their unique concept-cluster, can be seen to express the very opposite of what such negations usually imply. They denote the intrinsic fullness of the nature, not its vacancy or want. To wit, *"the essential nature is complete in itself, lacking nothing."*

So the clustering of negatives serves a philosophical purpose—disestablishing dogma, and loosening the hold of personal views and received opinions. It also has the psychological effect of stopping an outward-leaning dependence and, in its place, stimulating an inward examination and healthy self-reliance. Hence Huineng's parting verse,

> If you wish to cultivate, and aspire to become a Buddha,
> You won't know where to find this truth
> Unless you discover it within your own mind.
>
> I now leave behind the direct teaching.
> To become free, people must cultivate themselves;
> I announce to you and future seekers of the Way:
> If you fail to see this; you will miss it by a long, long way.

Third, the Sixth Patriarch himself provides interpreters with a connecting thread that binds together all the diverse parts: "My teaching never departs from the essential nature." Most of the text is dialogue between teacher and disciples; engaged, lively, concrete; not abstract treatise or third-person discourse. Through this dialogical back-and-forth, the Master illustrates and embodies the very nature of the Dharma: a raft for crossing over, not something to get a hold of and mindlessly cling to.

We know the Sixth Patriarch's teaching methods included sermons and question-and-answer exchanges both in public and private. Although he gathered around him a devout following of monks, nuns, and laity, all arrived independently, and remained or took their leave as the spirit moved them. His teaching skill was interactive and refreshingly non-didactic. Huineng apparently possessed an astute perceptual capacity, a mirror-like sensitivity that quickly and unfailingly revealed to him a person's mind in the very smallest of things. How the person bowed, what pleased or bothered them, an individual's tone of voice, a glance, an inflection or innuendo—all were like tiny loose threads that when tugged, revealed the warp and woof of the whole fabric.

By knowing the student, knowing their 'problem' or the particular 'knot' that he or she had gotten tied in, Huineng then could set about to expediently untie it. He does only what is called for by the situation, what is appropriate; no more, no less. True and false, right or wrong are specific, *in situ*, not abstract or absolutes. The Way is not bound to a prescribed set of beliefs; yet neither is it arbitrary and capricious. For Huineng, the "teaching" or Dharma was more like medicine prescribed to cure specific illnesses—one of the earliest Buddhist metaphors for *upaya* (*fang bian* 方便). The Dharma is only Dharma if it is appropriate—matched to the person, to the situation. Once the illness is cured, one can discontinue the medicine; once safe on the other shore, one can let go of the Raft. And as *The Lankavatara Sutra* reminds us: teachings that are not appropriate, are not the Teaching.

The closest we get to an absolute doctrinal statement from Huineng is the exhortation: 'let your mind be unattached; clinging to nothing.'

Yet even this is less a dogmatic utterance than a gentle reminder, an encouragement to not tie oneself up. He does *not* say "generate the thought that attaches to nothing" or "you must not be attached to things," as these would be already one step removed from the original mind which is of itself pure and still, lacking nothing and in no need of doing anything. He simply says, "Let it be" in its natural state, and do not move from one's own ground of liberated prajna, the non-dual, unattached original nature of human beings.

Even in his 'final instructions' he eschews doctrinal pronouncements in favor of practical instructions and words of encouragement.

> My teaching now is like the seasonal rains everywhere falling and moistening the earth. Your buddha-nature is like the seeds which sprout and grow when moistened by the rain.... The mind is fundamentally pure; with nothing to grasp or reject. Each of you work hard; and try your best wherever circumstances take you.

All translation is necessarily interpretation. And all interpretation is part objective, part personal. Context can never fully recover the historic 'then' in which it first occurred, nor can it ever escape the present 'now' in which it is being reimagined and revisited. Even more so with Buddhist texts where the contextual landscape is more demanding and difficult to navigate as it requires not merely linguistic tools and academic training, but intuitive tools acquired through spiritual training. The words of the Buddha must be reconstructed from documentary sources, but also from "living" sense. Edward Conze (1904–1979), the gifted Anglo-German scholar probably best known for his pioneering translations of Buddhist texts, many years ago pointed this out. "Buddhist texts," he observed, "are primarily spiritual documents, and the spirit alone can fathom them."

He argued "without meditation practice, these sublime records of wisdom teaching will easily turn into a string of lifeless absurdities."[7] The problem with treating a text like *The Platform Sutra* as an abstract philosophical treatise, or even as an exercise in philosophical reasoning misses its true import: a psychological catalyst and spiritually transformative device. It proffers not merely a new perspective, but promises to shift the very ground upon which we stand to observe.

For this understanding of Buddhist texts, we are forever indebted to our teacher, Master Hsüan Hua, who tirelessly lectured on the texts daily and encouraged us to master the languages required for translating these spiritual works. More importantly he nurtured and admonished us in the bittersweet work of self-cultivation so that we might directly get their meaning, not just their words, and in doing so, begin the real conversation the Zhuangzi epigraph alludes to. Master Hsüan Hua is the guiding light behind this translation and the enduring inspiration for all of our translations.

In China, translations of Buddhist materials from India and Central Asia took centuries to accomplish. The translations evolved and improved as the Chinese themselves evolved and matured in their inner understanding of the teachings. From the early stiff translations of An Shi Gao (c. 148 C.E.) over two hundred years passed before adequate equivalents started to emerge in the Chinese language, as with, for example, the exquisite renderings of Kumarajiva. We should not expect to arrive at Western English language translations any faster, despite our space-age communications technology. Technology can hasten the sharing and distribution of the sutras, but only a still mind can translate them.

---

7 Edward Conze, *Thirty Years of Buddhist Studies*. Bruno Cassirer Publishers Ltd. (1967).

Hundreds of years or more of study and practice will need to be put in before we arrive at suitable English translations that convey the idiomatic, dynamic, and 'therapeutic' equivalents of the original texts. We hope that this new rendering of *The Sixth Patriarch's Platform Sutra* in some small way advances this noble goal.

Rev. Heng Sure
Martin J. Verhoeven
Berkeley Buddhist Monastery
Berkeley, California
Spring 2014

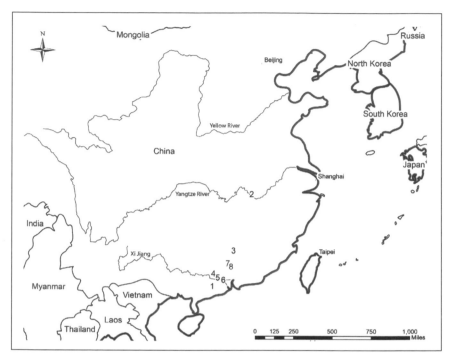

THE PLACES THE MASTER VISITED

1. Xinzhou: The birthplace of the Sixth Patriarch; also the location (Guoen Si) where the Sixth Patriarch passed away.

2. Dongchan Si: The home monastery of the Fifth Patriarch.

3. Dayu Ling: The barren and rocky locale where the Master converted Huiming.

4. Huaiji: The county where the Sixth Patriarch went into hiding.

5. Sihui: Where the Master lived among hunters for fifteen years.

6. Faxing Si: Monastery where the Master received full ordination.

7. Dafan Si: Temple venue of the Master's first large Dharma teaching; and the 'platform' from which the lectures in this Sutra were given.

8. Baolin Si: Main residence, where the Master lived and taught for thirty-seven years.

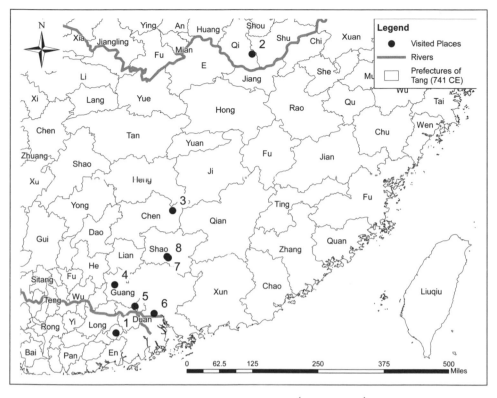

TANG PREFECTURES IN 741 (HARTWELL)

Available through the Worldmap open source platform developed by the Center for Geographic Analysis at Harvard University.

http://worldmap.harvard.edu/data/geonode:hw_0741_tang_pref_gb_09u

The map is provisional and it shows approximate prefectural boundaries in Tang dynasty, China in 741 C.E. The map is owned and shared by Dr. Peter K. Bol, the Charles H. Carswell Professor East Asian Languages and Civilizations at Harvard University.

Source: "Historical GIS of China, Robert G. Hartwell. Chinese Historical Software, Ltd, 1996. Distributed with CHGIS V2, under the auspices of Harvard Yenching Institute (2003)."

釋迦牟尼文佛

Na Mwo Original Teacher Sakyamuni Buddha

菩提達摩祖師

Twenty-Eighth Patriarch Arya Bodhidharma
The First Patriarch in China

慧可大師

Twenty-Ninth Patriarch Great Master Huike
The Second Patriarch in China

僧璨大師

Thirtieth Patriarch Great Master Sengcan
The Third Patriarch in China

道信大師

Thirty-First Patriarch Great Master Daoxin
The Fourth Patriarch in China

弘忍大師

Thirty-Second Patriarch Great Master Hongren
The Fifth Patriarch in China

惠能大師

Thirty-Third Patriarch Great Master Huineng
The Sixth Patriarch in China

A General Introduction

by Bhikshu Fahai of the Tang Dynasty[1]

The Great Master was named Huineng. His father's surname was Lu; his personal name was Xingtao. His mother's surname was Li. The Great Master[2] was born at midnight on the eighth day of the second month of the cyclical year Wuxu, in the twelfth year of the Zhenguan reign of the Tang Dynasty [638 C.E.]. During his birth, an effulgent light radiated through space and a rare fragrance filled the room.

At dawn, two foreign bhikshus came to visit. They said to the Master's father, "We have come to name the son born to you last night. He can be called Huineng."

The father asked, "Why should he be called Huineng?"

One of the bhikshus answered, "*Hui* [giving] means he will give the Dharma to all living beings. *Neng* [able] means he will be able to do the Buddha's work." Having said this, they left, and no one knew where they went.

The Master did not nurse; spiritual beings[3] came in the night to nourish him with sweet dew.

When the Master grew up and reached the age of twenty-four, he heard lines from a Sutra and realized a spiritual awakening. He then went to Huangmei to have his awakening confirmed.

---

1 Taken from Fahai's text collected in Roll 915 of the *Quantangwen* (全唐文). It is positioned here as front material; in other versions, it is appended at the end of the sutra.

2 Hereafter, simply 'the Master.'

3 Chinese is *shen ren* 神人.

There, the Fifth Patriarch measured his capacity and entrusted him with the robe and Dharma, making him the next Patriarch. This occurred during the first year of the Longxiang [alt. Longshuo] reign period, in the cyclical year Xinyou [661 C.E.]. He then returned to the south and went into hiding for sixteen years.

On the eighth day of the first month in the first year of the Yifeng reign period [676 C.E.], in the cyclical year Bingzi, he met Dharma Master Yinzong. (They engaged in a serious discussion about the deepest truths.[4]) Yinzong immediately grasped them and understood the Master's teaching.

The Master's head was shaved at a gathering of all the four assemblies, on the fifteenth day of that same month. On the eighth day of the following month, eminent and virtuous bhikshus gathered together to transmit the complete monastic precepts to him. They were:

Vinaya Master Zhiguang of Xijing, who served as Precept Transmitter.

Vinaya Master Huijing of Su Province, who was the Confessor Master.

Vinaya Master Tongying of Jing Province, who was the Teaching Transmitter.

Vinaya Master Qiduoluo of Central India, who recited the precepts.

Tripitaka Master Miduo of India was the Precept Certifier.

Construction of the precept platform had been initiated by Tripitaka Master Gunabhadra during the earlier Song Dynasty [420–477 C.E.]. He erected a stone tablet with the inscription, "In the future, a living Bodhisattva will receive the precepts in this very place."

4 Added from Taishō.

Moreover, in the first year of the Tianjian reign of the Liang Dynasty [502 C.E.], Tripitaka Master Jnanabhaishajya had come by sea from West India carrying a Bodhi-tree seedling, which he planted beside the platform.

He also prophesied that "After one hundred and seventy years, a living Bodhisattva will proclaim the Supreme Vehicle beneath this tree, crossing over multitudes beyond measure. He will be a true transmitter of the Buddha's 'mind-seal,' a Dharma Host."

In keeping with these earlier predictions, the Master arrived to have his head shaved and to receive ordination. He then instructed the four assemblies on the essence of the Dharma transmitted from generation to generation. (*From the cyclical year of Renwu, first year of Tianjian [502] of the Liang, until the cyclical year of Bingzi, first year of Yifeng [676] of Tang, it is one hundred and seventy five years.*)

In the following spring, the Master took leave of the assembly and returned to Baolin [Jewel-Wood Monastery]. Yinzong, together with more than a thousand black-robed monks and white-robed laity, accompanied him directly to Caoxi.

At that time Vinaya Master Tongying of Jing Province and several hundred students also followed the Master there to live with him.

When the Master arrived at Baolin, in Caoxi, he saw that the hall and buildings were bleak and cramped, inadequate to accommodate such a large group. Wishing to enlarge them, he visited a villager, Chen Yaxian, and said, "This old monk comes to the patron seeking a sitting cloth's worth of ground. Could that be arranged?"

Yaxian asked, "How big is the Master's sitting cloth?"

The Master then took out his sitting cloth to show it to Yaxian, who thereupon agreed. But when the Patriarch unfolded and spread out his sitting cloth, it completely encompassed the four borders of Caoxi. The Four Celestial Kings appeared and positioned themselves to protect the four cardinal directions. To this day, the mountain range bordering the monastery is called The Celestial King Range.

Yaxian said, "I know the Master's Dharma-power is profound, however, our ancestral burial ground lies on this land. If, in the future you build a stupa, I hope you will not disturb this burial parcel. I wish to donate the rest to remain a sacred site forever. This ground has the vital energy of a living dragon and a white elephant. Level only the high-ground, not the low."

Later, the monastery was built in accord with his wishes. The Master roamed these lands, and at places where the landscape was inspiring, he stopped to enjoy it. Accordingly, thirteen *aranyas*[5] were erected, which now comprise the present monastic complex of Huaguo.

The Baolin [Jewel-Wood] Bodhimanda itself was chosen long ago by Indian Tripitaka Master Jnanabhaishajya, who during his earlier journey from Nanhai, passed through Caoxi, where he cupped water into his hands for a drink. Tasting its sweetness, he told his disciples, "This water is just like the water in India. Its source would be an excellent location for a monastery."

Following the water to its source, he beheld the stream winding its way through the mountains with their impressive peaks and was moved to exclaim, "This looks just like Jewel-Wood Mountain in India!"

He told the Caoxi villagers, "You could build a monastery on this mountain. After one hundred and seventy years, an 'Unsurpassed Dharma Jewel' will teach here. Those who awaken here will number like the trees in this forest. It should, therefore, be called Baolin [Jewel-Wood]."

5 Sanskrit; a remote forest or uninhabited wilderness area ideal for hermits to practice Dharma.

At that time, the Magistrate of Shao Province, Hou Jingzhong, reported these prophetic words to the Emperor who responded favorably and conferred upon it the name Baolin Monastery, which was established in the third year of the Tianjian reign of the Liang Dynasty [504 C.E.].

In the front of the hall was a pond in which a dragon regularly sported, bumping and scraping the surrounding woods. One day he appeared, larger than ever, throwing up huge waves, and covering the area with a dense fog. The disciples were afraid. The Patriarch, however, scolded the dragon, saying, "Hah! You can only make yourself big, but not small. If you were a magical dragon, you could 'transform the small into the great and the great into the small.'" The dragon suddenly disappeared, only to return an instant later in a small body, skipping along the surface of the pond. The Master held out his bowl and teased him, saying, "You wouldn't dare climb into the old bhikshu's bowl!" Right then the dragon swam up to the Master, who scooped him out of the water with his bowl. The dragon could not move. With bowl in hand, the Master returned to the hall where he instructed the dragon in the Dharma. The dragon then shed his skin and departed. His skeleton, only seven inches long and complete with head, tail, claws, and horns, is preserved in the temple. Later the Master filled in the pond with earth and stones. An iron stupa now stands in that very place in front of the hall.[6] (Years later, the Dragon skeleton was lost due to a fire caused by warfare.)

---

6 The English translators chose 'in front of the hall' because the texts (Taishō vs. Quantangwen) vary according to one's vantage point; viewing it facing towards or facing away from the hall would situate it to one's right or left depending on position. 'In front of the hall' covers both.

CHAPTER ONE

Where It All Began

Once, when the Master arrived at Baolin [Jewel-Wood], the Prefect of Shao Province, Wei, whose given name was Qu, along with other local officials, climbed the mountain to invite the Master to come to the city so that he might give Dharma instruction to the people assembled in the lecture hall of Great Brahma Monastery [Dafan si]. After the Master was formally seated, the Prefect along with more than thirty other officials, more than thirty Confucian scholars, over a thousand Bhikshus, Bhikshunis, Taoists, and laity all bowed simultaneously to him and requested instruction on the essentials of the Dharma.

The Great Master said to the assembly:

> Good and Wise Friends, Bodhi is just the purity of your own nature. Attend only to this and you will straightaway achieve Buddhahood.
>
> Good and Wise Friends, listen; this is the story of how I came to realize the Dharma.
>
> My worthy father was a native of Fanyang, but he was banished to Xin Province in Lingnan where his status was reduced to a commoner. Unfortunately for me, my father died early, and as a result my widowed mother and I relocated to Nanhai where we were so miserably poor that I sold firewood in the market place for a living.
>
> Once, a customer bought firewood and had me deliver it to his inn where he took the wood and paid me. On my way out the gate, I noticed someone reciting a Sutra; as soon as I heard the words of the Sutra, my mind immediately awakened.[7]

7 Referring to the famous line from *The Diamond Sutra* where the Buddha instructs Subhuti, "Let your mind be unattached, clinging to nothing (*ying wu suo zhu, er sheng qi xin* 應無所住, 而生其心)."

I asked the person what Sutra he was reciting. He replied, *"The Diamond Sutra."* I then asked him, "Where are you from? Where did you get this Sutra?" He said, "I come from Eastern Chan [Dongchan] Monastery in Qi Province, Huangmei County. There the Fifth Patriarch, the Great Master Hongren, resides and teaches over a thousand disciples. I went there, bowed in respect, and encountered this Sutra. The Great Master constantly exhorts both the sangha and laity to simply cultivate according to *The Diamond Sutra,* so that they may by themselves see their essential nature and directly realize Buddhahood."

After hearing this, and because of a karmic connection from the past, I was given ten ounces of silver by another customer so I could provide my elderly mother with food and clothing. He told me to go right to Huangmei and bow to the Fifth Patriarch.

After making the necessary arrangements for my mother's welfare, I left right away and arrived in Huangmei in about thirty days. There I bowed to the Fifth Patriarch, who asked me, "Where are you from? What do you seek?" I replied, "Your disciple is a commoner from Xin Province in Lingnan. I come from afar to bow to you, and seek only to be a Buddha, nothing else."

The Patriarch said, "If you are from Lingnan, you must be a barbarian. How could you become a Buddha?!" I replied, "People may come from the north, or come from the south, but fundamentally there is no north or south to the buddha-nature.[8] The body of a barbarian and that of a High Master are not the same, but what difference is there in our buddha-nature?"

---

8 'Buddha' and 'buddha'. Upper-case "B" is used indicating the realized state of full-awakening. Lower-case "b" is used to indicate the potential for that awakening, as yet unrealized. Thus Buddhahood is capital "B"; buddha-nature is lower-case "b."

The Fifth Patriarch wished to continue the conversation, but noticing that his disciples were gathering all around, he told me to follow the group off to work. I said, "Huineng wants to inform the High Master that wisdom is always active in this disciple's mind, as I never depart from my essential nature—this itself is 'the field of blessings.' What work would the High Master have me do?" The Fifth Patriarch replied, "What a barbarian! You are very sharp. Say no more. Go to the granary shed in the back and get to work." So I withdrew to a back building where a laborer put me to work splitting firewood and threshing rice on the hulling pestle.

I spent more than eight months at this work, when the Patriarch unexpectedly came one day to see me, and said, "I think your insights can be of some use, but I was afraid that bad people would harm you. That is why I haven't spoken with you. Do you understand the situation?" I replied, "Your disciple understands the Master's intentions and has avoided the front hall so as not to call attention to myself."

One day the Patriarch summoned all his disciples and said to them, "I tell you, for all people the matter of birth and death is a serious concern. Yet all day long you just seek good fortune and happiness rather than trying to escape from the bitter sea of birth and death. If you are confused about your essential nature, how can blessings save you? I want all of you to draw upon your wisdom and use the prajna-essence of your original mind to compose a verse to show me. If you understand the great meaning, I will pass on to you the robe and Dharma, making you the sixth patriarch. Go now! This is an urgent issue. Thinking about it is useless—someone who has experienced the essential nature should see it immediately upon hearing these words! One who perceives like this could see it even in the heat of battle, facing whirling swords!"

The assembly received his instructions and withdrew, saying to one another, "We followers don't need to clear our minds and labor our wits to compose a verse to show the High Master. What's the use? Shenxiu is our senior instructor—certainly he will get it. It would be not only an affront to him, but a waste of effort for us to compose a verse."

Others hearing this, all put their minds to rest, saying, "From now on, we will rely on Master Shenxiu. Why worry ourselves composing verses?"

Shenxiu then thought, "The others are not submitting verses because I am their senior teacher. I must compose a verse to submit to the High Master—if I don't present a verse, how will the Master know the depth or shallowness of my insight and understanding? If my intention in submitting a verse is to seek for the Dharma, that is good. But if I covet the title of Patriarch, that is bad. How would that be any different from an ordinary person presuming to be a sage?! But, if I don't submit a verse, I will never get the Dharma. What a problem! What a problem!"

In front of the Fifth Patriarch's hall there was a corridor three rooms long, whose wall was to be frescoed by the Court Artist, Lu Zhen, with stories from *The Lankavatara Sutra* and a diagram of the lineage-succession of the five patriarchs, so that they might be venerated by future generations. After composing his verse, Shenxiu made several attempts to submit it. But whenever he reached the front hall, his mind was dazed and he broke out in a sweat. He made thirteen attempts over the course of four days, all unsuccessful. Then he thought, "It would be better to just write it on the wall so that the High Master might see it. If he says it's good, I will come forward, bow to him, and say, 'Xiu did it.' If instead he finds it unacceptable, then it means I will have spent my years on this mountain in vain, receiving veneration from others. Where would I go from there?"

That night, in the third watch (around midnight), so that no one would know, holding a candle he wrote his verse on the wall of the south corridor that would reveal his insight. The verse read:

The body is a bodhi tree,
The mind a mirror-stand bright.
Time and again, brush it clean,
And let no dust alight.

After writing this verse, Shenxiu returned to his room without anyone knowing what he had done. Then he thought, "If the Fifth Patriarch sees my verse tomorrow and is pleased, it will mean that I have an affinity with the Dharma. If he finds it unworthy, it will mean I am deluded, that karmic obstacles piled up from the past make me unfit to attain the Dharma. It is difficult to fathom a sage's intentions." He remained in his room, thinking it over, but could not sit or sleep peacefully the rest of the night, right through to dawn (the fifth watch).

Now, the Patriarch knew that Shenxiu had not yet 'entered the gate,' and seen his own essential nature. At daybreak, the Patriarch summoned the Court Artist, Lu Zhen, to fresco the wall of the south corridor. Suddenly seeing the verse, he said to the artist, "There is no need to paint anything; I am sorry we troubled you to come so far, but as *The Diamond Sutra* says, 'All forms are false and illusory.' Instead, leave this verse for people to recall and uphold. Whoever cultivates in accord with this verse will not fall into the evil destinies, and will obtain great benefit."

He then instructed his disciples to light incense and bow before the verse, and to recite it so they might see their essential nature. The disciples all recited it and exclaimed, "Excellent!"

At the third watch (around midnight), the Patriarch called Shenxiu into the hall and asked him, "Did you write this verse?" Shenxiu answered, "Yes, Xiu did it, but I dare not lay claim to the position of Patriarch. I only hope the High Master will be compassionate and see whether this disciple has any wisdom or not."

The Patriarch said, "Your verse shows that you have not yet seen your original nature;[9] you are still outside the gate and have yet to pass through it. With the views and understanding you have, you may seek for unsurpassed bodhi, but will not attain it. Unsurpassed bodhi means that right at the moment of speaking you are able to recognize your original mind, and see that your own fundamental nature is unborn and undying. Unsurpassed bodhi means you yourself see this naturally, at all times and in every instance of thought: that the myriad dharmas are of a piece, identical.[10] And that what is true of one, is true of all. The myriad phenomena are naturally 'thus' as they are. And a mind that is this way accordingly, is the true reality. To see in this way is the essence of supreme Bodhi. Go and think this over for a day or two. Then compose another verse and bring it to me. If you have 'entered the gate', I will entrust you with the Dharma robe and bowl."

Shenxiu bowed and left. Several days passed, but he was unable to compose a verse. His mind was in a daze, his spirit disturbed, and his mood anxious, as if he were in a dream. Whether walking or sitting down, he was miserable.

---

9 Chinese uses 'zi xing' 自性, 'ben xing' 本性, 'zhen xing' 真性, and just 'xing' 性 interchangeably to mean the same thing. In a similar fashion English uses 'inherent nature,' 'essential nature,' 'original nature,' 'fundamental nature' or just 'nature,' depending on the context.

10 wan fa wu zhi 萬法無滯 is a reference to the mind and its myriad objects as being one and the same, i.e. the myriad dharmas are 'mind-made,' or interactive with the mind; basically affirming non-duality of the mind and the 'reality' it 'creates.' See Eighteen Realms.

Two days later, a young acolyte passed by the threshing room while chanting Shenxiu's verse. Hearing it for the first time, I knew that the author had not yet seen his original nature. Although I had not yet received any formal teaching in the Dharma, I already understood its profound meaning. I asked the boy, "What is that verse you're reciting?" "Barbarian, you know nothing!" snapped the boy. "Don't you know that the Great Master has said that birth and death are the most urgent concern of all people? He wants to pass on the robe and Dharma, so he told his disciples to write verses and bring them to him for review. If anyone shows he has awakened to the profound meaning, he will inherit the robe and Dharma and become the Sixth Patriarch. Our senior, Shenxiu, wrote this unconditioned[11] verse on the wall of the south corridor. The Great Master ordered everyone to recite it, because whoever cultivates in accord with this verse can avoid falling into the evil destinies and gain immense benefit."

I said, *(one text adds "I too would like to recite it to create conditions for a favorable rebirth.")* Venerable One, I have been pounding rice here for over eight months and have yet to visit the front hall. Would you please lead me to the verse so I can pay homage to it?"

The boy then led me to the verse to bow. I said, "Huineng cannot read. Please, Venerable One, read it to me." An administrator of Jiang Province, a man called Zhang Riyong, happened to be there at the same time, and he read the verse aloud. After hearing it, I said, "I, too, have a verse. Will the official please write it down for me?" The administrator replied, "You, too, can compose verses? How unusual!" I replied to the official, "If you wish to study

11   Ch. *wu xiang* 無相; Skt. *animitta/nirabhasa:* 'markless/formless,' 'beyond material distinction or material reality,' thus 'unconditioned,' imparting something not conditioned by time, personality, place, history, i.e. true for all times and places, not subject to restrictions or true only for certain values, contexts.

the unsurpassed bodhi, do not slight a beginner. The lowest of the low may possess the highest wisdom. And the highest of the high may have the least wisdom. If you slight others, you create limitless, boundless offenses." The official then said, "Recite your verse, and I will write it out for you. If you gain the Dharma, you must liberate me first. Remember this. Don't forget what I say."

My verse went:

Basically, bodhi has no tree,
Nor any mirror-stand bright.
Originally there's not one thing:
Where could dust alight?

After this verse was written down, everyone was startled, amazed. They all said to one another, "How strange! You cannot judge a person by his appearance. How can it be that in such a short time one could become a living Bodhisattva?!"

The Fifth Patriarch, seeing everyone so excited, was worried that someone might harm me. He erased the verse with his sandal, saying, "This one, too, has not yet seen his nature." The whole community accepted this.

The following day, however, the Fifth Patriarch came unannounced to the threshing floor where I was pounding rice with a stone tied to my waist [for added weight]. He said, "A seeker of the Way would forget his very life for the Dharma. Isn't that so?" Then he asked me, "Is the rice ready yet?" I answered, "The rice has long been ready; it's only waiting now for the sieve." The Patriarch then struck his staff on the pestle three times and left. I immediately knew his intention, and at the third watch entered the Patriarch's room. Using his robe as a screen so that no one could see us, he explained *The Diamond Sutra* for me. And when he came to the line in the text, *"Let your mind be unattached, clinging to nothing,"*[12] as soon as these words were uttered I experienced a profound awakening, and understood that the inherent nature embraces the ten thousand things. I said to the Patriarch,

> *How unexpected! The essential nature is intrinsically pure.*
> *How unexpected! The essential nature is originally unborn and undying.*
> *How unexpected! The essential nature is complete in itself, lacking nothing.*
> *How unexpected! The essential nature is fundamentally still and unmoving.*
> *How unexpected! From the essential nature the myriad dharmas come to be.*[13]

The Patriarch realized that I had awakened to the essential nature, and said to me, "To study the Dharma without recognizing your original mind is useless. If you recognize your original mind, and see your essential nature, you can be called 'a great hero,' 'a teacher of gods and humans,' a 'Buddha.'"

I received the Dharma in the middle of the night and no one knew. At the same time the Master also entrusted me with the Direct Teaching and gave me the robe and bowl, saying, "You are the Sixth Patriarch. Be careful. Take across living beings everywhere.

12 *ying wu suo zhu, er sheng qi xin* 應無所住，而生其心; In *The Platform Sutra*, 'non-dwelling' and 'non-attachment' or 'not grasping/clinging' overlap and are used interchangeably, along with *wu nian* 無念, and *wu xin* 無心, which literally mean 'no-thought,' and 'no-mind.' All are different ways of expressing the same notion. Master Hsüan Hua, in his commentary to *The Diamond Sutra* says, "to have no-dwelling is to have no-attachment. No-attachment is liberation. Therefore, not-dwelling, one is liberated, independent, and not blocked or obstructed by anything."

13 See *Shastra on the Door to Understanding the Hundred Dharmas*, "myriad dharmas" or "10,000 dharmas," for a detailed explanation of *wan fa* 萬法.

Spread the teaching for future generations; don't let it be cut off. I have a verse for you:

Out of caring, I am planting this seed;
Because of the ground, the fruits will ripen again.
Without this feeling, there'd be no seed planted;
Without the nature, there'd be no new life to thrive.

The Patriarch further said, "Long ago, when the Great Master Bodhidharma came to this land, people did not believe in him. As a symbol of his sincerity, he bequeathed this robe to be passed along from generation to generation. The Dharma is handed down mind to mind leading all to their own awakening and their own liberation. From ancient times, all Buddhas only transmit the fundamental truth; the true intention is passed along more privately from master to master. The robe, however, has become a source of contention; let it stop with you and not be passed on. For if you pass it on, your life will be hanging by a thread. Quickly go now, for I fear others might harm you!" I asked, "Where should I go?" The Patriarch replied, "Stop at Huai, and hide at Hui."[14]

In the third watch, I received the robe and bowl, and asked, "I am a Southerner and do not know these mountain roads. How do I get to the mouth of the river [Yangtze]?" The Fifth Patriarch said, "Don't worry. I will see you off myself." The Fifth Patriarch escorted me as far as the Jiujiang courier station, where he had us get on a boat. The Patriarch took up the oars and began to row. I said, "Please, Master, sit down. Your disciple should row." The Patriarch replied, "It is appropriate that I take you across." I said, "When someone is confused, his master takes him across. But when one

14 Huai 懷 is a district in Guangdong; Hui 會 is another location, now called Xinhui in Guangdong.

has awakened, he takes himself across. Both are called 'crossing over,' but they are used differently. I was born in a border region, so my speech has an accent, yet I have been entrusted with the Dharma. And now that I have awakened it is only right that I 'take across' my own essential nature." The Patriarch replied, "So it is, so it is. From now on, because of you the Buddhadharma will flourish. Three years after you depart, I will leave this world. Start on your journey now and go south as quickly as possible. Don't be in a hurry to teach; the Buddhadharma is hard to propagate."

After I took leave of the Patriarch, I set out on foot southward. Within two months I reached the Dayu Mountains. (The Fifth Patriarch returned to the monastery, but did not enter the hall for several days. The community was concerned and went to ask: "Has the Master some slight illness or problem?" The Master replied, "I am not ill; but the robe and Dharma have already gone south." They asked, "Who was it entrusted to?" The Patriarch answered, "The 'able one' obtained it." The community then knew who this was.)

Soon several hundred of them set off in pursuit, all hoping to steal the robe and bowl. One Bhikshu, Huiming, whose lay surname was Chen, was a rough and coarse-natured man who had once been a general. He was intent on finding me and chased me down before anyone else. Just as he caught up with me, I discarded the robe and bowl onto a rock, hid in the underbrush, and said, "This robe and bowl are tokens of trust. How can they be seized by force?!" Huiming went over to the robe and bowl and tried to pick them up, but he could not move them. He cried out, "Cultivator, cultivator! I have come for the Dharma, not for the robe."

I then came out and sat on a boulder. Huiming bowed and said, "I hope the cultivator will teach me the Dharma." I said, "If you have come for the Dharma, then clear your mind of all thoughts and I will teach you." Huiming was quiet for a long while. I said, "Before a thought of good or a thought of evil—right at that moment, what is venerable Ming's original face?" When Huiming heard these words he experienced a profound awakening. Huiming then questioned me further, asking, "Other than the secret words and secret meaning you just uttered, is there yet another secret meaning?" I answered him, "What I just told you is not a secret. If you look within yourself, you'll find the 'secret' is with you."

Huiming said, "Although Huiming was at Huangmei, he had never actually paid attention to his original face. Now, with your instruction I am like a man who takes a drink of water and knows for himself whether it is hot or cold. Cultivator, now you are my master."

"If you feel that way," I said, "then you and I have the same Master of Huangmei. Protect and maintain it well." Huiming then asked, "Where should I go now?" I said, "Stop at Yuan; stay at Meng." Huiming bowed and departed.

(Returning to the foot of the mountain, Huiming said to the crowd of pursuers, "Up above there are only rocky, trackless heights; there's no trace of him to be found. We should search elsewhere." The pursuers all agreed. Afterwards, Huiming changed his name to Daoming, to avoid using the first name of his master.)

Later I came to Caoxi, but was again pursued by evil men. So I fled to Sihui where I lived among hunters for fifteen years, occasionally teaching them the Dharma when the opportunities arose. The hunters had me watch over their snares, but whenever I saw living creatures, I released them. At mealtime I steamed vegetables in the pot alongside the meat. If they asked me about this sometimes, I'd say, "I only eat the vegetables cooked alongside the meat."

One day I thought, "The time has come to spread the Dharma. I cannot stay in hiding forever. Accordingly, I went to Dharma Essence [Faxing] Monastery in Guang Province where Dharma Master Yinzong was lecturing on *The Nirvana Sutra*. At that time there was a pennant waving in the breeze. One monk there said, "The wind is moving." Another monk said, "The pennant is moving." They argued on this incessantly. I stepped forward and said, "It is not the wind that is moving, nor is it the pennant that is moving. It is your minds that are moving, Kind Sirs." Everyone was startled.

Dharma Master Yinzong invited me up to the dais [seat of honor] where he questioned me closely about the deeper meaning behind my words. He noticed that my responses were direct, concise, and did not come from written texts. Yinzong said, "This cultivator is certainly no ordinary person. Long ago I heard that the Dharma robe and bowl of Huangmei had come south. Might you be that one, cultivator?" I replied, "I dare not presume such a thing."

Yinzong bowed and asked me to show the robe and bowl I was entrusted with to the community. He questioned me further, "How exactly was Huangmei's teaching transferred?" I replied, "There was no transfer. We merely discussed seeing the nature. There was no discussion of dhyana Samadhi or liberation." Yinzong asked, "Why was there no discussion about dhyana Samadhi or liberation?" I said, "Because those are dualistic teachings, not the Buddha-Dharma. The Dharma of the Buddha is a non-dual Dharma." Yinzong further asked, "What is this Buddha-Dharma you call the Dharma of non-dualism?" I answered, "The Dharma Master has been lecturing *The Nirvana Sutra*'s elucidation of the buddha-nature—this is the non-dual Dharma of the Buddha-Dharma. Just as when Lofty Virtue King Bodhisattva asks the Buddha, 'Do those who break the four major prohibitions, or commit the five rebellious offenses, or who are *icchantikas*[15] and the like, sever their roots of goodness and the buddha-nature?' And the Buddha replies, 'There are two kinds of roots of goodness: permanent and impermanent. The buddha-nature, however, is neither permanent nor impermanent.' Therefore, it cannot be severed. That is what is meant by non-dual. The first [kind of roots] are good; the second, not good. But the buddha-nature is neither good nor bad. That is what is meant by non-dual. Ordinary people think of the skandhas and sense-realms[16] as dualistic. The wise person knows that they are non-dual in nature. The non-dual nature is the buddha-nature."

Yinzong was overjoyed when he heard this explanation. He put his palms together and said, "My explanation of this sutra is like broken clay tiles; whereas your explanation of its meaning, Kind Sir, is like pure gold." He then shaved my head and asked me to be his teacher. Thus, under that Bodhi-tree, I first began the East Mountain (Dongshan) teaching.[17]

I had received the Dharma at East Mountain and had endured such extreme hardship that my life was hanging as if by a thread. Today there's this gathering of the Prefect and officials, the bhikshus, bhikshunis, Taoist priests and laity—how could this happen without karmic affinities amassed over eons of time?

And now you have had the good fortune to hear the Direct Teaching, the seed for realizing the Dharma. All of this can only be because in the past you made offerings to the Buddha and planted roots of goodness.

15 Sanskrit term for those lacking any potential for awakening; one who has cut off all wholesome roots (Skt. *kushala*) in him or herself.

16 There are eighteen 'sense-realms': the six sense faculties of seeing, hearing, smelling, tasting, touching, and the thinking-mind; and six sense-objects: sights, sounds, scents, flavors, tangible objects, and ideas; and the six consciousness which arise between them.

17 'first began' meaning after coming out of fifteen years of hiding.

This teaching has been passed down from sages of the past; it is not my own wisdom. You who wish to comprehend the teaching of the past sages should purify your minds. After listening to it, cast aside your doubts, and you will be no different from the sages of generations past.

Delighted with what they had heard, the whole assembly bowed and withdrew.

CHAPTER TWO

Prajna

The following day Prefect Wei asked for further instruction. The Master ascended to the lecture seat and said to those assembled:

> You should all clear your minds and focus your attention on the Great Perfection of Wisdom (Maha-prajnaparamita).

He then said:

> Good and Wise Friends, all people originally possess the profound knowledge of Bodhi and Prajna within them, but they cannot realize it themselves because their conditioned minds wander and become confused. That is why they must rely on a Good and Wise Advisor who can lead them to see their intrinsic nature.
>
> You should know that the buddha-nature is fundamentally no different for the foolish and the wise. The only difference between them is: the foolish are confused; the wise are awakened.
>
> I will now explain the teaching of the Great Perfection of Wisdom for you, so that each of you may become wise. Pay careful attention and listen well as I explain it.
>
> Good and Wise Friends, people chant "prajna" all day long without realizing the prajna of their own essential nature. Just as talking about food will not satisfy hunger, so too only talking about emptiness, even for myriad eons, will give you no insight into your own nature—ultimately it is of no benefit.
>
> Good and Wise Friends, *Maha-prajnaparamita* is a Sanskrit phrase which means "great wisdom that goes to the other shore." This must be practiced with the mind; not merely recited by the mouth.

Verbal repetition without mental cultivation is like a fantasy, a hallucination, like dew drops and a lightning flash.[18] If, however, while the mouth recites, the mind practices, then both mind and mouth are in accord. One's own essential nature is Buddha; apart from this nature there is no other Buddha.

What does *Maha* mean? *Maha* means "great." The capacity of the mind is vast and far-reaching; like empty space, it has no boundaries. It is neither square nor round, large nor small. Nor is it blue, yellow, red, or white. It has no above or below, no long or short. Moreover, it has no anger or joy, right or wrong, good or evil, beginning or end.

All Buddha-lands are ultimately the same as empty space. The wondrous nature of people is originally empty; there is nothing that can be grasped. And the true emptiness of the essential nature is the same.

Good and Wise Friends, do not listen to me explain emptiness, and then become attached to emptiness. Above all, do not cling to emptiness. If you meditate with a vacant mind, you will become fixated on a blank emptiness.

Good and Wise Friends, the emptiness of the physical universe can embrace the shapes and forms of the myriad things: the sun, moon, and stars; the mountains, rivers, and the whole earth; the fountains, springs, streams, and torrents; the grasses, trees, thickets, and woods; good and bad people, good and bad dharmas, the heavens and the hells, all the great seas, and the entirety of Mount Sumeru and all mountains—empty space contains them all. The emptiness of people's nature is the same.

---

18 An allusion to *The Diamond Sutra* passage "All conditioned dharmas / Are like dreams, illusions, bubbles, and shadows / Like dew drops and a lightning flash / One should contemplate them in this way."

Good and Wise Friends, our own essential nature is able to contain the "ten thousand things"—this is "great." The myriad dharmas, absolutely everything, are within the nature of all people. If you can regard all people, the bad as well as the good, without grasping or rejecting, free of any clinging, your mind will be like empty space. Thus, it can be called "great," *Maha*.

Good and Wise Friends, confused people only mouth the words; wise people actually practice with their minds. Moreover, there are deluded people who empty their minds while sitting in quietude, without thinking anything whatsoever, and declare this "great." It is worthless to talk with such people, because theirs is a wrong view.[19]

Good and Wise Friends, the capacity of the mind is great and far reaching; it encompasses the Dharma Realm. When functioning, it is clear and distinct, discerning and responsive. It knows all. All is the one [the mind]; and the one [mind] is all.[20] Things naturally come and go, but the essence of the mind is unimpeded. That is *Prajna*.

Good and Wise Friends, prajna wisdom comes from one's own essential nature: it does not come from outside. Do not make the mistake of using will and intellect. It is called "The natural workings of the true nature." When the self-nature is true, everything else is true.

The mind has the capacity for great things; it is not meant to behave in petty ways. Do not talk about emptiness all day long, but fail to cultivate it in your minds. That would be like a commoner

19 'wrong view' Ch. *xie jian* 邪見; Skt. *drsti*; erroneous views, ideas, opinions influenced by craving, aversion, and delusion, that obstruct insight and awakening.

20 The 'one' and 'everything' here refers to the mind and all its associated states; not to be construed as a vague mystic apprehension of 'unitary consciousness,' pantheism, or other notions of 'cosmic consciousness.'

proclaiming himself the king of the country. How absurd; this could never be! Such people are not my disciples.

Good and Wise Friends, what is prajna? In our language, prajna means wisdom. In every place and in every moment, in thought after thought, never becoming muddled and constantly acting wisely—just this is practicing prajna.

With one deluded thought, prajna is cut off. With one wise thought, prajna springs to life. Ordinary people, muddled and confused, fail to recognize prajna. Their mouths talk about prajna, but their minds remain confused. They are forever saying, "I cultivate prajna!," and though they talk on and on about emptiness, they have no idea of its true meaning. Prajna has no shape or form; it is only the mind of wisdom. If you understand it in this way, just this is prajna wisdom.

What does *paramita* mean? This is a Sanskrit word; in Chinese it means "arriving at the other shore." It means that one is no longer bound by birth and death. If one clings to the sensory realm, birth and death arise, like waves arise on water—this is called "this shore." If you do not cling to sensory states, there is no birth and death, just like freely flowing water—this is what is meant by "the other shore." So, it is called paramita.

Good and Wise Friends, confused people recite with their mouths, yet right while they recite, they live in falsity and error. To cultivate in every moment of thought—that is the true nature. Understand this Dharma; it is prajna Dharma. And cultivate this practice; this is living the life of prajna. If you fail to cultivate in this way, you will just be an ordinary person. But the moment you put it into practice, you yourself are equal to the Buddhas.

Good and Wise Friends, ordinary people are themselves Buddhas, and affliction[21] itself is bodhi. In one past moment of confused thought you are just an ordinary person. If the very next thought is awakened, you are a Buddha. Previous thoughts clinging to sensory states are afflictions; and succeeding thoughts unattached to states is bodhi.

Good and Wise Friends, Maha-prajnaparamita is the most honored, the most supreme, the foremost. It does not dwell, it does not come or go. All Buddhas of the past, present, and future emerge from this.

You should use this great wisdom to see through the defiling afflictions of the five skandhas.[22] Those who cultivate in this way are certain to realize the awakening of the Buddha, transforming the three poisons into morality, contemplative calm, and insight.

Good and Wise Friends, in this teaching of ours 84,000 wisdoms flow from this one Prajna. Why? Because people have 84,000 kinds of affliction. Free of defiling affliction, wisdom constantly and naturally manifests, as it is inseparable from one's inherent nature. Those who understand this teaching know it is not intellectual thinking; not remembering or recalling to mind; is free of any grasping or clinging; and is not in the least false or deceptive.

Use your own true nature and [its inherent] wisdom to contemplate and illuminate all dharmas without grasping or rejecting them. Just this is seeing one's essential nature and realizing Buddhahood.

---

21 Chinese *fan nao* 煩惱; Skt. *klesa*; inclinations and tendencies, often lying deep in the mind, that cause mental, emotional, and physical distress and agitation. They hinder practice and obstruct awakening. They are rendered under a wide range of names: 'afflictions,' 'defilements,' 'hindrances,' 'yokes,' 'outflows,' 'raging streams,' 'fetters,' 'arrows,' 'jungle,' 'entanglement.'

22 The five 'heaps' or 'aggregates' (Skt. *skandhas*) which collectively constitute the human individual. They are: form, feelings, perception, mental 'actions' and impulses, and consciousness. These psycho-physical phenomena are not a permanent, stable, eternal and unchanging soul/self (which is nowhere to be found), but a series of five transitory, suffering, impersonal 'aggregates' ever subject to change and rebirth.

Good and Wise Friends, if you wish to enter the most profound Dharma Realm and the samadhi of Prajna, you should cultivate the practice of Prajna, and recite by heart[23] *The Diamond Prajna Sutra*. Then you will be able to see your own essential nature. You should realize that the merits of this Sutra are incalculable, measureless, as clearly described in the Sutra text itself; but nobody could explain this fully.

This teaching is the Supreme Vehicle, expounded for people of great wisdom and superior faculties. When people of limited faculties and wisdom hear it, they doubt and disbelieve. Why? By analogy, it is like the rain that magical dragons shower on Jambudvipa that washes away all the cities, towns, and villages as if they were mere leaves and straw. But rain falling on the ocean causes the ocean neither to increase nor decrease. Similarly, when people of the Great Vehicle, the Supreme Vehicle, hear *The Diamond Sutra* explained, their minds are receptive; they awaken and understand. They realize that their fundamental nature is in itself replete with the wisdom of Prajna. They constantly use this wisdom to contemplate and to illuminate; they do not need to rely on the written word.

This wisdom is like rainwater, which does not really come from the sky. In truth the dragons engender the rains whose moisture enriches all living beings, all plants and trees—all those sentient and insentient beings. The hundred streams flow together into the ocean, and there merge into a single body. The wisdom of Prajna, the fundamental nature of living beings, is also like this.

23 *chi song* 持誦; meaning more like 'memorize,' 'get by heart.'

Good and Wise Friends, people of limited capacities who hear this direct teaching[24] are like plants and trees with shallow roots which collapse under heavy rain and are unable to grow. So it is with people of small capacities: they fundamentally have the wisdom of Prajna, no different from people of great wisdom. Yet, why don't they awaken on their own when they hear this teaching? It is because obstacles of their wrong views are formidable and the roots of their afflictions go deep.

It is like when thick clouds obscure the sun; if the wind doesn't blow, the sun cannot shine.

Prajna wisdom is itself neither great nor small. But living beings differ because their own minds are either awakened or confused. Those with confused minds who look outwardly in their cultivation in search of the Buddha have not yet awakened to their essential nature; just this is "small roots."

If you have awakened to the Direct Teaching, you do not cultivate by grasping at externals. You simply uphold right views constantly in your own mind; the defiling passions never stain you. Just this is "seeing the self-nature."

Good and Wise Friends, if you can cultivate a mind that does not cling to anything inside or outside, and comes and goes freely, such a mind that can get rid of all grasping gains unhindered understanding—this is to be one and the same with *The Diamond Sutra*.

Good and Wise Friends, all the sutras[25] and writings of the Great and Small Vehicles, and the twelve divisions of the canon—all these

---

24 *dun jiao* 頓教; often translated as 'sudden teaching' in contrast with 'gradual.' From here on translated as 'direct' to convey its meaning as 'immediate,' lit. not 'mediated' by any expedient teaching, techniques, or stages. Thus 'direct' contrasts with 'provisional.' Here 'direct' means stemming immediately from and returning to a source; straight; without any intervening diversion or steps.

25 *xiuduoluo* 修多羅, Chinese transliteration of Sanskrit "*sutra*."

were established because of people—and could only have been set up because of [their] wisdom nature.

If there were no people in the world, all the myriad Dharma-teachings would not exist by themselves.

Therefore, you should realize that the myriad Dharma-teachings arise because of people, and all Sutras are taught and explained for people.

Because some people are deluded and some are wise, the deluded being the small and the wise being the great, the deluded question the wise and the wise teach Dharma for the deluded.

When the deluded suddenly understand and their minds awaken, then they are no different from the wise.

Good and Wise Friends, unawakened, Buddhas are just living beings. At the moment they awaken, however, living beings are Buddhas. Therefore, you should realize that the ten thousand dharmas are all within your own mind. Why don't you immediately see, right within your own mind, the true reality of your original nature?

The Bodhisattva-sila Sutra[26] says, "Our original, fundamental essential nature is pure." If we but recognize our own mind and see our nature, we will all certainly realize Buddhahood.

The Vimalakirti Sutra says, "Just here and now, regain your original mind."

Good and Wise Friends, when I was with the Venerable Master Hongren, I awoke as soon as I heard his words and immediately saw my original nature as it truly is.

---

26 *pusajie jing* 菩薩戒經, literally means "The Bodhisattva Precepts," and is actually the 10th Chapter of a larger text, *The Brahma Net Sutra*. It is sometimes, however, considered a sutra in its own right.

That is why I am conveying this teaching and practice, so that students of the Way may directly awaken and realize Bodhi. Each of you look into your own mind; see your original nature yourself.

If, however, you are unable to awaken on your own, you must seek out a Good and Wise Teacher, someone who understands the Dharma of the Supreme Vehicle, and who can show you the right way.

A Good and Wise Teacher who has the background and an affinity [with you] can transform and guide you, leading you to see your original nature. This is because the good and wise teacher is able to stimulate all good dharmas.

All Buddhas of the past, present, and future, as well as the twelve divisions of sutras are originally inherent, whole and complete, within human nature. If you cannot understand on your own, you must seek out a Good and Wise Advisor who can lead you to see. If you are someone who can awaken on your own, however, do not seek outside. Don't think that I am saying that you can only gain liberation through a Good and Wise Teacher, other than yourself. That is mistaken. Why? Within your own mind there is a good advisor who can awaken you yourself.

But if you let yourself morally stray, become confused, confounded, and all mixed up with wrong thinking, then even if a Good and Wise Advisor gives you instruction, he will not be able to help you. If you return to what is correct and true, use Prajna to contemplate and illuminate, then in an instant all confused thinking will vanish. If you recognize your essential nature, in one moment of awakening you will attain the stage of a Buddha.

Good and Wise Friends, when you contemplate and illuminate with a wisdom that clearly penetrates both inside and outside, you can discern your original mind. Recognizing your original mind is the fundamental liberation. And this liberation is itself the Prajna Samadhi; this is no-thought.

What is no-thought? If you can view all dharmas with an unattached mind, this is no-thought. The mind is everywhere engaged but is nowhere attached.

Just purify your original mind so that the six consciousnesses go out the six [sensory] "gates," yet remain undefiled and do not intermix with the six "dusts" [sensory objects], coming and going freely, penetrating without obstruction. This is the Prajna Samadhi, freedom and liberation. This is the practice of no-thought.

If you do not think of anything at all in order to repress and eradicate thought, this is called "Dharma-bondage." It is an extremist view.

Good and Wise Friends, one who realizes the Dharma of no-thought thoroughly comprehends the myriad things. One who realizes the Dharma of no-thought sees the realms of the Buddhas. One who realizes the Dharma of no-thought reaches the stage of Buddhahood.

Good and Wise Friends, later generations who encounter my Dharma should take up this Direct Teaching, and together with those of like minds and like practice vow to maintain it as if they were attending on the Buddha. To the end of their lives if they do not retreat, they will definitely join the ranks of sages.

Pass it along in this way from generation to generation; impart it carefully and with discretion. Don't conceal the genuine teaching, yet do not transmit it to those whose attitudes and practices hold to other teachings, since it could be harmful, and ultimately of no benefit. I fear that deluded people may misunderstand and revile this teaching, and in doing so cripple their inherent potential for Buddhahood for thousands of lifetimes.

Good and Wise Friends, I have an unconditioned verse which you should all recite and take to heart. Whether you are a monastic or layperson, just cultivate in accord with it. It will be of no benefit at all, however, if you yourself do not cultivate, but only memorize my words. Here's a verse for you:

Thoroughly understanding in both speech and mind,
Like the sun abiding in the empty sky,
Just spread this teaching: "seeing the nature,"
Manifest in this world, destroy false teachings.

Now, the Dharma is neither immediate nor gradual,
It is only confusion and awakening that are quick or slow;
But deluded people just cannot grasp
This "seeing the nature" teaching.

Although it can be explained in myriad ways,
If it accords with truth, they are ultimately one.
In the dark house of the afflictions,
Always keep burning bright the sun of wisdom.

When the false comes, the afflictions come,
When the true comes, the afflictions go.
False and true both put to rest,
Is purity supreme, purity without remainder.

Bodhi is our original, inherent nature;
Stir up the mind, and it all goes wrong.
Yet the pure mind is right within the false:
Just stay in the true, the three hindrances vanish.

If people of the world cultivate the Way,
Nothing at all can hinder them;
Always recognize your own faults,
And you will be in accord with the Way.

Each form has its own Path
They do not hinder or trouble one another.
If you abandon the Way to seek a by-path,
To the end of your days you'll never see the Way.

A frantic passage through life
Will end in bitter regret,
If you wish to discover the true Way—
Right practice is the Way.

If you do not have a mind for the Way,
You are stumbling in the dark; blind to the Way;
Someone who truly walks the Way,
Is blind to the faults of the world.

If you point out others' faults,
Your fault-finding itself is a fault;
Others' faults I do not fault,
As for my own faults, I blame myself.

Just get rid of the fault-finding attitude;
Once cast aside, the afflictions vanish;
When attraction and aversion no longer block the mind,
Stretch out both legs and lie down.

If you hope to teach and transform others,
You yourself must have the skillful means;
Do not raise doubts in others,
And their essential-nature will manifest by itself.

The Buddha Dharma is right here in the world,
There is no awakening apart from this world;
To search for Bodhi somewhere beyond this world,
Is like looking for a rabbit with antlers.

True-seeing is world-transcending,
False-seeing is the 'worldly';
False and true both set aside:
The bodhi-nature naturally appears.

This verse is the Direct Teaching;
It's also called the 'Great Ship of Dharma';
Confused, you might listen for ages;
Unconfused, you get it in an instant.

The Master further said:

Here now in the Great Brahma Monastery I have explained the Direct Teaching. I hope that all living beings throughout the Dharma Realm, upon hearing this will see their nature and realize Buddhahood.

At that time everyone who was listening to the Master's explanation—Prefect Wei, the officials, Taoists, and laity—all experienced an awakening. They bowed in unison to the master and exclaimed with delight, "Outstanding! Who would have ever expected that in Lingnan a Buddha would appear in the world!"[27]

27 Lingnan was a large area that included the monastery as well as the Master's home after his father was banished to Lingnan, and where his father's status was reduced to 'commoner.'

CHAPTER THREE

Doubts and Questions

One day, Prefect Wei hosted a large vegetarian feast on behalf of the Master. After the meal, the Prefect asked the Master to ascend the dais [take the formal lecture seat]. Along with the officials, scholars, and assembled people, he respectfully bowed and asked, "Your disciple has listened to the Master's explanation of the Dharma. It is truly inconceivable, but I now have a few doubts, and hope you will be compassionate and resolve them for me."

The Master said, "If you have any doubts, then ask, and I will explain them for you."

Prefect Wei said, "Isn't what you lectured to us the same teaching as Bodhidharma's?"

The Master replied, "It is."

The Prefect said, "I have heard that when Bodhidharma first taught the Emperor Wu of the Liang, the emperor asked, 'All my life I have built temples, sponsored monastic ordinations, made donations, and arranged vegetarian feasts. What merit and virtue have I gained?' Bodhidharma said, 'In fact, there was no merit and virtue.' Your disciple does not understand the principle here; please Master, explain it for us."

The Master answered:

> There truly was no merit and virtue; do not doubt the words of the ancient sage. Emperor Wu's attitude was wrong; he did not understand the correct Dharma. Building temples, sponsoring Sangha ordinations, making donations, hosting vegetarian feasts—all of this is called "seeking blessings." But blessings should

not be mistaken for merit and virtue. Merit and virtue are to be found in the Dharma body, not in cultivating blessings.

The Master continued:

Seeing one's essential nature is merit; equanimity is virtue. To be flexible and unimpeded in thought after thought, always cognizant of the true and wondrous workings of one's original nature—this is called "merit and virtue."

Inwardly, your mind humble, is merit; outwardly, your behavior respectful, this is virtue. Establishing the myriad dharmas from your own self-nature is merit, yet keeping your essential mind free from [wrong] thought is virtue. Not departing from one's essential nature is merit; actively responding without being affected is virtue. If you would seek the merit and virtue of the Dharma body, just live by these principles, for this is genuine merit and virtue.

People who cultivate merit and virtue harbor no thoughts of belittling others; instead they show respect to all. If you are always slighting others in your heart, and are constantly self-centered, then you have no merit. If your own nature is vain and false, you lack any virtue. It is only because they consider themselves to be great that they always belittle others.

Good and Wise Friends, [cultivating] continuously in thought after thought is merit; an unbiased, sincere, straightforward mind is virtue. Self-cultivation of one's own nature is merit; cultivation of one's own person is virtue. Good and Wise Friends, merit and virtue must manifest from within your own nature; do not seek for them by making donations and offerings. That is the difference between blessings, and merit and virtue. Emperor Wu did not understand this principle. Our Patriarch was not in error.

The Prefect further asked, "Your disciple often sees the sangha and laity reciting 'Amitabha Buddha' hoping to be reborn in the West [in the Pure Land]. Please explain this for me: will they actually gain rebirth there? Please resolve my doubts."

The Master said:

Prefect, listen carefully; I will explain it for you. When the World-Honored One was in the city of Sravasti, he taught about the Western Pure Land as an inducement to practice. The text of the Sutra clearly states, "It is not far from here." In discussing this, it might appear that it is 108,000 miles away; but it just means that the ten evils and eight wrongs are right within ourselves. Describing it as distant is meant for those with limited capacity. Saying it is nearby is for those with greater ability.

There are two kinds of people, not two kinds of Dharma. Awakening and confusion differ only because discerning may be quick or slow. Deluded people recite the Buddha's name seeking rebirth elsewhere; awakened people purify their own minds. That is why the Buddha said, "As the mind is purified, the Buddhaland is purified."

Sir, even a person of the East is blameless if he simply purifies his mind. However, even a person of the West is at fault if his mind is not pure. When a person of the East does wrong, he recites the Buddha's name hoping for rebirth in the West. But when a person of the West does wrong, in what country could he seek to be reborn by reciting the Buddha's name? Ordinary deluded people, unaware of their essential nature, do not realize that the Pure Land is within themselves. So, they long to be born in the East, and they long to be born in the West. To the enlightened person all places are the same. As the Buddha said, "No matter where you are, you are always happy and at ease." Good Sir, if the ground-of-the-mind is free of anything unwholesome, the West will not be very far away. If you invoke the Buddha's name yet still hang on to unwholesomeness, it will be hard to gain that rebirth [in the Pure Land].

Good and Wise Friends, I exhort you now: first get rid of the ten evils;[28] in doing so you will have walked one hundred thousand miles. Next, eliminate eight wrongs[29] and you will have covered another eight thousand miles. If in every moment of thought you keep your essential nature in view, and if in everything you do you are even-minded, true and direct, then in a finger-snap you will arrive there and see Amitabha.

Good Sir, if you just practice the ten good deeds,[30] then why would you further need to seek rebirth there? But if you do not rid your mind of the ten evils, what Buddha would come to welcome you? If you awaken to the eternal, direct Dharma, you will behold the West [the Pure Land] in an instant. Without awakening to this, you might recite the Buddha's name seeking rebirth there, but the road is so long—how could you ever traverse it? I will move the West here in an instant so you can see it right before your eyes. Would you all like to see it, or not?

The entire assembly bowed and said, "If it could be seen right here, why would we vow to be reborn there?! Please, Master, be compassionate; make the West appear for all to see."

28 Ten evils (Skt. *dasa-akusala-karmapatha*); they are: 1) killing; 2) stealing; 3) sexual misconduct; 4) lying; 5) slandering; 6) harsh speech; 7) idle talk and gossip; 8) greed; 9) hatred; and, 10) wrong views.

29 *ba xie* 八邪, 'the eight wrong practices or paths.' The opposite of the Noble Eightfold Path to awakening (Ch. *ba zheng dao* 八正道; Skt. *ārya-aṣṭāṅgika-mārga*: Right View, Right Thought, Right Speech, Right Action, Right Livelihood, Right Effort, Right Mindfulness, and Right Concentration.)

30 Ten good deeds (Skt. *dasa-kusala-karmapatha*); they are: 1) not to kill; 2) not to steal; 3) to avoid sexual misconduct; 4) not to lie; 5) avoid slandering; 6) avoid harsh speech; 7) refrain from idle talk and gossip; 8) non-greed; 9) non-hatred; and, 10) right views.

The Master said:

All of you here, a person's own physical body is the city [of the Pure Land], and the eyes, ears, nose, tongue [and physical body] are its gates. The city is thus made up of five outer entrances, and an additional inner gate—the gate of consciousness.[31] The mind is the ground; and one's nature is the king. The king dwells on the mind-ground, and as long as the essential nature is present, the king is present. But when the nature departs, there is no king. When the nature is present, the body and mind are well cared for, but when the nature leaves, the body (and mind) fall apart.

Buddhahood is realized within the essential-nature; do not seek for it outside yourself. Confused, the self-nature is a living being; enlightened, the self-nature is a Buddha. Kindness and compassion are Avalokiteshvara; sympathetic joy and equanimity are Mahasthamaprapta. Purifying [oneself] is Shakyamuni; and, to be unprejudiced and free of guile is Amitabha.

Egoism and arrogance are Mount Sumeru. Sensual desires are the oceans' waters, and the afflictions are its waves. Cruelty is an evil dragon; vanity and dissoluteness[32] are the ghosts and spirits; worldly passions are the fish and turtles; lust and hatred are the hells; and, delusion is the animals.

Good and Wise Friends, always practice the ten good deeds and you can easily reach the heavens. Get rid of egoism and arrogance, and Mount Sumeru topples. Eliminate sensual desires and the oceans' waters dry up. When the afflictions cease, the waves calm. When cruelty is ended, the fish and turtles are no more. The enlightened

---

31 'consciousness' refers to what is called the 'sixth consciousness' (Skt. *mano-vijnana-dhatu*).

32 *xu wang* 虛妄, close to English meaning 'vain and dissolute', i.e. lacking restraint, indulging, lit. 'dissolve.'

nature of the Tathagata radiates an effulgent light on the ground of your own mind. Outwardly, this light illuminates the six gates, and its purity can penetrate through the six desire-heavens. Inwardly, it illumines the essential nature and dispels the three poisons, and retributions like the hells vanish in an instant. Inside and outside are clear through and through—no different from the Western Land. But if you do not cultivate in this way, how could you ever go there?!

Hearing his explanation, the assembly clearly recognized their essential nature. They all bowed and in near-unison exclaimed, "How fine! May all living beings of the Dharma Realm who hear this simultaneously awaken!"

The Master said:

Good and Wise Friends, if you wish to cultivate [this practice] you can do it at home—you do not have to be in a monastery. If you can cultivate at home you are like the person of the East whose mind is good; conversely, being in a monastery but not cultivating is like the person of the West whose mind harbors evil. Just purify your mind; that is the "West" of your essential nature.

Prefect Wei further asked, "How can this be practiced at home? Please teach us."

The Master replied:

I will recite an unconditioned verse for you. As long as you practice in accord with it, you will be as if always by my side. However, if you do not cultivate, then what benefit in your search for the Way is shaving your head [tonsure] and taking ordination? Here is the verse:

The mind regulated and subdued, why toil following rules?
Your "steps" straight and true, what use is sitting in meditation?

Gratitude: being filial and supporting your parents;
Righteousness: being sympathetic to those above and below.

Deference: high and low showing mutual respect;
Patience: not gossiping about everyones' wrongs.

If rubbing sticks can spin smoke into fire,
Then a red-petalled lotus can surely spring from the mud.

Good medicine is bitter to the taste;
Good advice often hurts the ears.

Reforming your failings gives birth to wisdom;
Excusing and defending them shows a petty mind.

Persist daily in being generous and forgiving;
Donating money, however, cannot bring enlightenment,

Search out Bodhi only in the mind,
Why waste effort seeking outside in the occult?

Just practice according to these words,
And "paradise" will appear right before your eyes.

The Master then added:

Good and Wise Friends, all of you should cultivate according to this verse. Take hold of your essential nature and directly realize Buddhahood. Time waits for no one. This gathering has ended; it is time to leave. I will return to Caoxi. If anyone has doubts, then come and ask me about them.

On this occasion the Prefect, government officials and staff, as well as the good and sincere men and women in the assembly all gained a deep understanding which they sincerely embraced and put into practice.

CHAPTER FOUR

Concentration and Wisdom

The Master addressed the assembly:

Good and Wise Friends, this Dharma teaching of ours is rooted in concentration and wisdom. Don't be confused and say that concentration and wisdom are different. Concentration and wisdom are of one essence, not two. Concentration is the essence of wisdom, and wisdom is the functioning of concentration. Where there is wisdom, concentration exists right within that wisdom. Where there is concentration, wisdom exists right within the concentration. If you grasp the meaning of this, you know that wisdom and concentration are complementary and studied together.

Students of the Way, do not say that these two are different, either with concentration preceding and producing wisdom, or with wisdom preceding and producing concentration. Holding this view implies the Dharma is dualistic. If you speak good but are not good at heart, then your wisdom and concentration are useless because they do not align with each other. If, however, your mind and talk both are good, and inside and outside are the same, then concentration and wisdom are one and the same.

The cultivation of self-awakening is not a subject for debate. If you argue about which comes first, which comes after, then you are just as deluded as everyone else. If you do not put a stop to contention [literally, "victory and defeat"], then you only inflate your sense of "self," and will not break away from the "four appearances."[33]

Good and Wise Friends, what are concentration and wisdom like? They are like a lamp and its light. If there is a lamp, there is light; without a lamp, there is darkness. The lamp is the essence of the light; and the light is the functioning of the lamp. Although they go by two different names, fundamentally they are identical. The phenomenon of concentration and wisdom are also like this.

The Master said to the assembly:

Good and Wise Friends, the Single-Practice Samadhi means always maintaining a direct mind in all situations, whether walking, standing, sitting, or reclining. As *The Vimalakirti Sutra* says, "The direct mind is the place of awakening; the direct mind is the Pure Land."

Do not allow the workings of your mind to become twisted, while merely talking about directness with your mouth; nor expound on the Single-Practice Samadhi but fail to cultivate the direct mind. Just cultivate with a direct mind and do not cling to anything. The deluded person, seizing on the appearance of things, latches onto the Single-Practice Samadhi, saying, "I constantly sit unmoving and my mind never stirs. This is the Single-Practice Samadhi!" But those who interpret it in this way render themselves insensate, and create conditions that obstruct the Way.

Good and Wise Friends, the Way should be open and free-flowing. How could it be impeded?! When the mind does not cling to anything,

33 *laksana*, also *nimitta*; *avastha*; four states/marks of all phenomena: birth, being, change/decay, and death; or birth, life, aging, death; or initiation, continuation, change, and cessation. Also refers to: 1) the illusion that there is a real "self" in the skandhas 2) that this "self" is an "I" or personality different from other beings 3) that living beings have a "self" that is born of the skandhas 4) that this "self" has a fated or limited life.

the Way accordingly circulates and flows. The mind that clings to dharmas ties itself up; it's called "self-bondage." If you say that always sitting without moving is correct, then you are like Sariputra who was scolded by Vimalakirti for sitting quietly in the forest.

Good and Wise Friends, there are also people who teach sitting, gazing into the mind, contemplating tranquility, without moving or getting up. They claim this will produce good results. Confused people, lacking discernment, grab onto this practice and go mad. There are many such people. You should understand that these kinds of teachings are really off, mistaken.

The Master instructed the assembly:

Good and Wise Friends, the correct teaching is basically neither "direct" nor "gradual"; it is people's dispositions that are sharp or dull. The deluded person who cultivates gradually, and the more aware person who [cultivates] directly, converge: each recognizes their original mind, each sees their original nature. In this, they are the same. Therefore, "direct" and "gradual" are just provisional terms.

Good and Wise Friends, this teaching of ours from its very inception has taken freedom from thought as its source, freedom from appearances as its essence, and freedom from clinging as its basis.

"Freedom from appearances" means to be detached from appearances while in the midst of appearances. "Freedom from thought" means detachment from thought in the midst of thought. And, "freedom from clinging" is the basic nature of human beings. In this world of good and evil, beauty and ugliness, enemies and friends—even during times when one meets with insults, criticism, verbal attacks, bullying—treat all of this as empty and harbor no thoughts either of delight or of revenge. In each continuing moment of thought do not dwell on previous thoughts. If you think about the previous thoughts, the present thought, and take up future thoughts, then your thoughts will continue without cease. This is bondage. If in each continuing moment of thought you do not cling to anything at all, this is freedom from bondage. This is the meaning of "not-clinging is our basis."

Good and Wise Friends, remaining detached from all outward appearances is called "freedom from forms." If you can stay detached from forms and appearances, then dharmas are essentially pure. This is the meaning of "freedom from forms is the essence."

Good and Wise Friends, when the mind remains undefiled within all sensory states, this is called "freedom from thought." In your thoughts you are always impassive and detached from sensory states; you do not rouse your mind over them. If, however, you do not think of anything at all [literally, "the hundred things"], and completely eradicate thought until the last thought entirely ceases, you will die and be reborn in some other place. Students of the Way take heed; this is a big mistake.

If you cannot recognize your own mistaken interpretation of the Dharma, how much more will you mislead others! You do not even see your own confusion, and discredit the Buddha's sutras. That is why we establish "freedom from thought" as our source.

Good and Wise Friends, why do we take "freedom-from-thought" as our core principle? Because there are deluded people who claim to have seen their essential nature, yet their minds get stirred up over sensory states. They then create wrong views based on these thoughts, and from this all kinds of afflictions and misunderstandings are generated. In our own essential nature there is basically not a single thing that can be grasped. To hold that there is something to get [leads to] reckless talk of failure and success, and then to afflictions and wrong views. Therefore, our teaching establishes "freedom-from-thought" as its source and core doctrine.

Good and Wise Friends, "freedom from" means free from what? And "thought" means thought of what? "Freedom from" means a mind free from any trace of duality, and one free from every mental defilement. Thought [thus freed] is thinking that comes from one's true and ultimate original nature. This "being-thus" true nature is the essence of thought; and thinking is the functioning of this "being-thus" true nature. Such thinking is activated from the true reality of the essential nature's "true-being." The eyes, ears, nose, and tongue cannot think. Rather, it is from the essential-nature's true "being-thus" that thought arises. Without it, the sense organs and their corresponding forms and sounds would scatter and break down.

Good and Wise Friends, this thought flows from the essential nature's true reality. Although the six sensory faculties see, hear, feel, and know, the [essential nature] is not affected by the myriad sensory states; your true nature is eternally free and independent. Therefore *The Vimalakirti Sutra* says, "One who can skillfully discern the characteristics of all dharmas, remains solid and firmly grounded in the deepest truth."

CHAPTER FIVE

Sitting Meditation

The Master said to the assembly:

The practice of sitting meditation basically consists of not fixating on the mind, nor on purity, nor is it just sitting motionless. If you speak of "fixing on the mind," this mind is fundamentally false. You should realize that the mind is like an illusion, with nothing at all to grab onto.

You might say it [sitting meditation] is fixating on purity, yet people's nature is basically pure. Only because of confused thinking is its natural true "thus-being" obscured. Only put an end to your confused thinking, and the nature is pure of itself.

If you attach to an idea of purity, you will only end up with a false sense of purity. It is a delusion, unreal. This attachment is wrong. Purity has no shape or appearance, and yet there are those who create the appearance of purity and consider it skilled meditation. This attitude only covers over your own original nature; you become entangled in purity.

Good and Wise Friends, someone who cultivates not-moving, when he observes other people does not notice their rights or wrongs, good or bad sides, or their faults and failings. Just this is the unmoving, essential nature.

Good and Wise Friends, deluded people might make their bodies immobile, but as soon as they open their mouths they gossip about others' rights and wrongs, their good qualities and shortcomings— and in doing so, they turn their backs on the Way. So, if you fixate on the mind and cling to purity, this just obstructs the Way.

The Master continued:

Good and Wise Friends, what does "sitting meditation" mean? To engage in this practice means you remain unhindered and unobstructed. Your mind and thoughts do not stir no matter what good and bad state or external situation presents itself. That is called "sitting." And to inwardly discern the unmoving stability of the essential nature—this is called "meditation."

Good and Wise Friends, what does "meditative concentration" mean? Remaining detached from external appearances is called "meditative." Remaining inwardly undisturbed is called "concentration." If you attach to external appearances, inwardly your mind will become restless and confused. If, however, you remain unfazed by appearances, inwardly your mind will be unperturbed. The essential nature is naturally pure and still, but becomes confused when we let our thoughts chase after the things we see. If, no matter what situation we encounter, our mind remains unconfused, this is true concentration.

Good and Wise Friends, outwardly detached from appearances is "meditative," and being inwardly unconfused is "concentration." This combined outward detachment and inner lack of confusion, is meditative concentration. *The Bodhisattva Precepts Sutra* says, "Our original nature is inherently pure."

Good and Wise Friends, in every moment of thought never lose sight of the purity and clarity of your own original nature. You yourself must cultivate, practice and realize the Buddha Way!

CHAPTER SIX

To Repent and Renew

At that time, seeing the gentry and villagers from all over the Guang and Shao regions had gathered at the mountain monastery to hear the Dharma explained, the Master took the formal lecture seat and addressed the assembled crowd.

Welcome, each of you Good and Wise Friends! This work [i.e. self-cultivation] must begin right where you are in your everyday life. At all times, in every moment of thought, purify your own mind, cultivate yourself and work on yourself. See for yourself your own Dharma-body and the Buddha within your own mind. Liberate yourself; regulate and train yourself—only then will you have not come here in vain.

You have come from afar to gather here together; this is because we share in a karmic connection. Now, all of you kneel upright and I will first confer the Five Dharma-body Incenses of the inherent nature, and then the unconditioned Repentance and Renewal.

The assembly knelt, and the Master said:

First is the incense of morality: this is simply your own mind blameless, free from evil, envy and jealousy, without greed and anger, thieving or harm—this is called "the incense of morality."

Second is the incense of concentration: this is simply your own mind remaining clear and undisturbed in the midst of all conditions, good or bad—this is called "the incense of concentration."

Third is the incense of wisdom: this is simply your own mind unhindered by anything, but always using wisdom to contemplate and illuminate the essential nature, and never allowing any evil to set in. One does all kinds of good, but attaches to nothing; is respectful and considerate toward young and old alike, sympathetic towards orphans and the destitute—this is called "the incense of wisdom."

Fourth is the incense of liberation: this is just your own mind independent and free of self-seeking; not deliberating over good and evil; unhindered and at ease—this is called "the incense of liberation."

Fifth is the incense of liberated knowledge and understanding: this is just your own mind unaffected by anything good or bad, neither sinking into emptiness nor clinging to meditative stillness. Study extensively, be learned and well read; recognize your original mind and master the Buddhas' teachings. Graciously welcome and get along with all creatures; have no notion of "self" and "other." Directly reach Bodhi, your unchanging true nature—this is called "the incense of liberated knowledge and understanding."

Good and Wise Friends, these incenses emit a redolence within each of you. Do not seek outside.

I will now transmit an unconditioned repentance liturgy, so you may remove the wrongs you have done, are doing, and might do, and purify the "three karmas of body, mouth, and mind."

Good and Wise Friends, repeat after me:

May I from the preceding moment of thought, the present moment of thought, and in the following moments of thought, in every moment of thought, be free of any stupidity and confusion; I now completely repent of all previous stupidity, delusion, and unwholesome, unskillful karma done in the past, and may their effects be wiped away, and may I never do them again.

*May I from the preceding moment of thought, the present
moment of thought, and in the following moments of thought, in
every moment of thought, be unstained by arrogance and deceit.
I now completely repent of all previous unwholesome, unskillful
karma I have created out of arrogance and deceit in the past.
May their effects be wiped away, and may I never do them again.*

*May I from the preceding moment of thought, in the present
moment of thought, and in the continuing moments of thought,
in moment of thought to moment of thought, be unstained
by jealousy and envy. I now completely repent of all previous
unwholesome, unskillful karma I have created out of jealousy
and envy. May their effects be wiped away, and may I never do
them again.*

Good and Wise Friends, the foregoing is the unconditioned
Repentance and Renewal liturgy. Why is it called "to repent?" Why
is it called "to renew?" "Repent" means to regret so thoroughly
of all unwholesome karma done previously and motivated by
stupidity, confusion, arrogance, deceit, jealousy, envy, and other
unwholesome tendencies, that they never recur. That is "to repent."

"To renew" means to turn back from such wrongs; it means from
now on you have awakened to the stupidity, confusion, arrogance,
deceit, jealousy, envy and other unwholesome tendencies, have
reversed course and will never revert to them again. This is "to
renew." Together, it is called "to repent and renew."

Ordinary people, who are deluded and confused only think to
repent of their former errors. They do not know to renew and start
over by refraining from committing them again, so the wrongs
of the past are not really wiped away, and they will only keep

repeating these errors in the future. So, with past errors not wiped away, and future errors continuing to be created, how could this be considered "repenting and renewing?"

Good and Wise Friends, now that you have repented, I will teach you how to make the four great all-encompassing vows. Listen carefully:

> Though the living beings of my own mind are limitless, I vow to liberate them all.
> Though the afflictions of my own mind are limitless, I vow to change them all.
> Though the Dharma teachings of my own nature could never be exhausted, I vow to learn them all.
> Though the Buddhahood of my own nature is unsurpassed, I vow to realize it.

Good and Wise Friends, all of you just said, "I vow to liberate the limitless living beings of my own mind." But what does that mean? It does not mean that I, Huineng, liberate them!

Good and Wise Friends, the "living beings" within your own mind are the deluded thoughts, deceitful and untrue thoughts, unwholesome thoughts, jealous thoughts, malicious thoughts—all mental states like these, are "living beings." Each must be liberated from within your own nature. This is true liberation.

What is meant by liberating yourself through your own essential nature? It means liberating the living beings of false views, the afflictions and delusions within your own mind by means of right views. Once you have right views, you use the wisdom of prajna to lay bare and untangle [your] mistaken, confused and deluded "living beings." You yourself liberate each and every one. When falseness occurs, liberate it with truth; when confusion arises, liberate it with awakening; when delusion sets in, liberate it with wisdom, when evil takes hold, liberate it with goodness. Liberation like this is true liberation.

Further, "I vow to change the limitless afflictions" means using the prajna wisdom of your own essential nature to rectify the vain and dissolute impulses and ideas of your own mind.

Further, "I vow to learn the inexhaustible Dharma teachings," means to discern your own nature and always act on true principle. This is true learning.

As for "I vow to realize unsurpassed Buddhahood," this is just always cultivating what is true, appropriate, and right with a humble attitude. You sustain a prajna that is beyond delusion or awakening, and the [relativities of] true and false, but instead, see the buddha-nature directly, and realize the Buddha's awakening effortlessly, immediately. The power of these vows lies in constant mindful cultivation.

Good and Wise Friends, now that you have made the four encompassing vows, I will confer upon you the unconditioned precepts of the Three Refuges.

Good and Wise Friends, return to the awakened, doubly-complete honored one. Return to what is genuine and true, the honor and dignity of freedom from desire.

Return to what is pure, the honored and esteemed among the multitudes.[34] From this day forward, call "awakening" your teacher, and never again take refuge with demonic cults and outside Ways.

---

34 An allusion to the Sangha, a religious community of people who have received the full precepts and properly ordained. *The Anguttara-nikaya* says, "The community of the Buddha's followers walks the Way well, honestly, truthfully, and correctly. Thus it is composed of those who have accomplished the eight arya [noble] stages of effort and attainment to realize sagehood. The community merits veneration, respect, offerings, and respectful greetings from ordinary people, for it is a supremely rich field that yields a rich harvest to all people."

Constantly use the three treasures of your essential nature to verify and confirm [what is true]. Good and Wise Friends, I exhort you all to take refuge in and return to the three treasures of your own essential nature:

The Buddha is awakening.
The Dharma is what is right and true.
The Sangha is purity.

When your own mind takes refuge in awakening, error and delusion do not occur. The lessening of desires brings contentment, and you can free yourself from wealth and sensuality. This is called "the doubly-complete honored one."

When your own mind takes refuge in what is right, appropriate, and true, in every moment of thought there are no wrong views. Lacking any wrong views, there is no selfish egotism, no arrogance, craving and clinging. This is called "the honored one free from desire."

When your mind takes refuge with purity, your own essential nature is completely unattached and unstained by any state of longing and desire. This is called "the honored one esteemed among the multitudes."

If you cultivate in this way, this is taking refuge with yourself.

Ordinary people fail to understand this, and so from morning to night they take the Three Refuge Precepts. You say you take refuge with the Buddha, but where is the Buddha? If you do not recognize the Buddha, how can you return to him? Such talk is absurd.

Good and Wise Friends, each of you examine yourself. Do not go about this incorrectly. The sutra [*Avatamsaka*] clearly says you should return and rely on your own Buddha, not with some other Buddha. If you do not return to the Buddha within, there is nothing you can rely on. Now that you have awakened yourselves, each of you take refuge with the three treasures of your own mind. Inwardly, regulate your mind and character; outwardly, respect others. This is to take refuge with yourself.

Good and Wise Friends, now that you have taken refuge with the three treasures of your own [nature], each and everyone listen carefully as I explain for you the Buddha of our own inherent nature as a single essence with three bodies. This will enable you to discern the three bodies and completely awaken to your own inherent nature by yourself.

Follow me in saying:

I take refuge with the pure Dharma-body [Skt. *Dharmakaya*] within my own body.

I take refuge with the perfect, complete Reward-body [Skt. *Sambhogakaya*] within my own body.

I take refuge with the hundreds of thousands of myriad Transformed-bodies [Skt. *Nirmanakaya*] within my own body.

Good and Wise Friends, the physical body is an inn you cannot return to or rely on.

These three bodies exist within our nature; all people of this world have them. But because they are confused and do not see the inner nature, they seek externally for the Tathagata's bodies. They do not realize that they have the three bodies of the Buddha within their own bodies.

You should all listen to what I am saying, for it will allow you to recognize that right within your own body, your own nature is replete with the three bodies of a Buddha. These three bodies arise from your own essential nature; they do not come from outside.

What is the pure Dharma-body Buddha? People's essential nature is basically pure and from it the ten thousand things are created. Thoughts of evil give birth to evil deeds; thoughts of goodness give birth to wholesome deeds. Thus it is that all dharmas come to be from the essential nature. It is like the sky above which is always clear, and the sun and moon which are forever bright. Even if they are obscured by floating clouds that overshadow the world below in darkness, the sky above remains clear. If a wind suddenly comes up, scattering the clouds, then above and below are both bright, and everything reappears and becomes visible. The tendency of people is to constantly drift like the clouds in the sky.

Good and Wise Friends, insight is like the sun, and wisdom is like the moon. Insight and wisdom are always bright, but if we attach to external things, the floating clouds of errant thoughts cover over our essential nature so it is obscured and cannot shine. If you meet a Good and Wise Advisor, and hear the genuine and true Dharma, you can get rid of your confusion, so that inside and out are thoroughly clear and the myriad phenomena of the essential nature are all manifest. That is how it is with those who see their own nature. This is called the "pure Dharma-body of the Buddha."

Good and Wise Friends, when your mind takes refuge with your own essential nature, it takes refuge with the real Buddha. "Self-refuge" means getting rid of all unwholesome states of mind: all jealousy and envy, flattering and fawning, egotism, lying and deceit, contempt, rudeness and disrespect, bias and distortion, arrogance, and all other unwholesome tendencies whenever they arise. Always recognizing your own faults and not gossiping about others' rights and wrongs, is taking "self-refuge." Always humble and respectful—just this is the unobstructed seeing of the essential nature. This is taking "self-refuge."

What is the perfect, complete Reward-body of the Buddha? Just as one lamp can disperse a thousand years' darkness, one insight can wipe out ten thousand years' delusion. Do not think about the past; it is gone and can never be recovered. And do not keep thinking about what is yet to come. Instead, with every moment of thought perfect and clear, see your original nature. Though good and evil differ, the original nature is non-dual. That non-dual nature is the real nature. This real nature, unstained by either good or evil, is called the "perfect, complete Reward-body of the Buddha." If a single thought of evil arises within the essential nature, it destroys ten thousand aeons of good karma. One good thought generated from the essential nature erases evils as many as the sands of the Ganges River. To reach unsurpassed Bodhi directly, discern this in every moment of thought and do not lose your fundamental mindfulness. This is the "perfect, complete Reward-body of the Buddha."

What are the "hundreds of thousands of myriad Transformed-bodies of the Buddha?" If your thoughts do not get caught up in the myriad things, then your nature is basically like empty space.

But, with a single thought, "transformation" occurs. Evil thoughts transform into hell-beings [Skt. *naraka*]; wholesome thoughts transform into divine-beings [Skt. *devas*]. Viciousness is transformed into snakes and dragons; compassion transforms into Bodhisattvas. Wisdom transforms into the higher realms; delusion into the lower realms. The transformations of the essential nature are extremely numerous. The deluded person, however, does not understand this truth, and so continually creates evil in thought after thought and goes astray. If they would turn back a single thought to goodness, they would give birth to wisdom: this is called the "Transformed-body of the Buddha" within your essential nature.

Good and Wise Friends, the Dharma-body of the Buddha is fundamentally complete, lacking nothing. To see your essential nature yourself in every moment of thought is the "Reward-body of the Buddha." The thoughts generated by the Reward-body are the Transformed-body of the Buddha. You yourself awakening and cultivating the merit and virtue of your essential nature is genuine "taking refuge." The physical body is made of skin and flesh; it is just an inn you stay in and do not return to. Just awaken to the three bodies of your essential nature and you will recognize the Buddha of your own nature.

I have an unconditioned verse for you. If you can memorize and live by it, it can, the moment it is spoken, melt away the delusion and errors of accumulated aeons. The verse goes:

Confused people cultivate blessings, not the Way;
They just say "cultivating blessings is the Way."
The blessings of charity and donations may be boundless,
But the three poisons are rooted in the mind.

Fostering blessings to wipe away errors,
May bring future blessings, but the errors still remain.
Just rid yourself of unwholesome states of mind—
Self-nature's true repentance and return.

Suddenly you realize the true repentance of the Great Vehicle:
Get rid of the false, keep the true, do no wrong.
To learn the Way, look within, observe your own essential nature;
Then you are one and the same with each and every Buddha.

Our Patriarchs passed along this Direct Teaching,
Wishing that all might see the nature and together gain the Way.
If you wish to see the Dharma-body in the future,
Detach yourself from the appearances of things, and cleanse
your mind.

Strive to see it for yourself; don't just waste your time—
When your last thought ceases, so does your life.
Awaken to the Great Vehicle; see your inherent nature;
Reverently, respectfully, seek it with all your heart.

The Master said:

Good and Wise Friends, everyone should memorize this verse and cultivate by it. If you can see your nature right while these words are uttered, then even if we are a thousand miles apart, you will be always at my side. If you do not awaken to these words, then face-to-face, we are a thousand miles apart—so why did you bother coming so far to see me?! Take care; go well.

The entire assembly who heard this teaching gained a profound understanding, and joyfully put it into practice.

CHAPTER SEVEN

Lively Encounters

BHIKSHUNI WUJINZANG

After the Master received the Dharma teaching in Huangmei, he returned to Caohou village in Shao Province where no one knew him. *(Another text says, "When the Master left for Huangmei he went to the village of Caohou where he stayed for more than nine months." The Master earlier had said [in Chapter One], however, that he arrived in Huangmei in about thirty days. How could he be so determined to seek the Way, yet linger [in Caohou] for more than nine months!? So the time given in this other version is incorrect.)* There, a Confucian scholar, Liu Zhilue, graciously received the Master. Zhilue's aunt, Wujinzang (Inexhaustible Treasure), was a bhikshuni [Buddhist nun] who constantly recited *The Mahaparinirvana Sutra*. After listening to it for a while, the master grasped its wondrous meaning and began to explain it to her.

Scroll in hand, the nun then asked about some of the words. The Master replied, "I cannot read the words; please ask about the meaning." The nun said, "If you cannot even read the words, how can you understand the meaning?!" The Master answered, "The subtle meaning of all Buddhas has nothing to do with words and language." The nun was amazed and informed the village elders, "This man has realized the Way. We should ask him to stay and accept our offerings and support." A certain Cao Shuliang, who was the great-great-grandson of a Wei dynasty [220–266 C.E.] *(another version lists 'Jin' as the dynasty)*[35] Martial Lord, eagerly came, along with the local residents, to pay homage to the Master.

35 There were at this time multiple overlapping claimants to the dynastic throne based on differing geographic locations.

Now at that time, the ancient monastery of Baolin [Jewel-Wood], which had lain in ruins since being burned in the wars at the end of the Sui dynasty [589–617 C.E.], was rebuilt on its old foundation, and the Master was invited to stay there. He soon turned it into a sacred center. The Master lived there for nine months, when he was once again pursued by an evil mob. The Master hid in the mountains in front of the monastery, but they set fire to the woods and underbrush. He escaped by crawling among the rocks and concealing himself there. One rock still bears the imprint of the Master's knees and the outline of his robe where he sat in the lotus meditation position. Because of this, it has come to be known as "Escape Rock." Remembering the Fifth Patriarch's instructions to "stop at Huai, and hide at Hui," he went to these two locations, where he lived in hiding.

BHIKSHU FAHAI

The bhikshu [Buddhist monk] Fahai was from Qujiang in Shao Province. When he first called on the Master, he asked, "Will you please instruct me on the line: 'The mind itself is Buddha'?"

The Master answered, "When your preceding thought is not formulated, this is 'mind itself'; and when your following thought is not extinguished, this is 'Buddha.' Setting up in appearances is 'mind'; and being free from them is 'Buddha.' If I were to explain it fully, I would never finish, even if I spoke until the end of time. Listen to my verse:

> *The mind itself is called wisdom,*
> *Buddha is just concentration.*
> *Consciousness is clear and pure,*
> *When concentration and wisdom unite.*
>
> *To understand this teaching,*
> *You must work on your own nature—*

It's been here all along.
Both should be cultivated together.

At these words, Fahai had a deep awakening. He spoke a verse in praise:

The mind itself is Buddha,
I am embarrassed I didn't understand.
Now I know the source of concentration and wisdom:
I cultivate both together; and cling to nothing.

BHIKSHU FADA

Bhikshu Fada [Dharma Penetrating] was from Hong Province. He had left home to become a monk at the age of seven, and constantly recited *The Lotus Sutra*. When he came to pay homage to the Master, he bowed but did not touch his head to the ground. The Master[36] scolded him, saying, "If you bow without touching the ground, isn't that like not bowing at all?" You must have something on your mind. What is your practice?"

He said, "I have recited *The Lotus Sutra* over three thousand times already."

The Master said, "It doesn't matter if you recited it ten thousand times. If you understood the Sutra's meaning, you would not be so overbearing, and might be a fellow cultivator with me. You have applied effort in vain, yet don't even understand how wrong you are. Listen to my verse:

The point of bowing is to lower the banner of pride;
So why don't you touch your head to the ground?
When your ego is in the way, offenses will arise,
But when you forget your achievement, then blessings are supreme.

36 Hereafter alternately referred to as either the "Master" or the "Patriarch."

The Master asked further, "What is your name?"

"Fada," he answered.

The Master said, "Your name means 'Dharma Penetrating,' but what Dharma have you penetrated?!" He then spoke this verse:

Your name means "Dharma Penetrating,"
And you diligently recite without cease,
You recite in vain, mouthing empty words,
But one who knows his mind is a bodhisattva.

Because we have a karmic connection,
I will now explain it to you:
Place your trust in a Buddha beyond words;
And lotuses will bloom from your mouth.

Hearing this verse, Fada remorsefully said, "From now on I will respect everyone. I, your disciple, have been reciting *The Lotus Sutra* without understanding its meaning, and have always harbored doubts. Venerable Master, your wisdom is deep and vast. Will you please explain the essentials of this sutra for me?"

The Master said, "The Dharma is profoundly penetrating, but your mind has not penetrated it. There is nothing doubtful in the sutra; the doubts are in your mind. You recite this sutra, but what do you think its core teaching is?"

Fada replied, "This student is dull and slow. All along I have only recited by rote, so how could I understand its main purport?"

The Master said, "I cannot read, but if you recite it for me, I will explain it to you."

Fada then recited the sutra aloud. When he came to the chapter on Parables, the Master said:

Stop there! The central teaching of this sutra has always been about the reasons why the Buddha appears in this world. All of its parables address this. What are these reasons? The sutra says, "All Buddhas, the World-Honored Ones, appear in the world because of the One Great Matter." The One Great Matter is the knowledge and vision of the Buddha.

Ordinary people, confused about the external world, attach to appearances; confused inwardly, they cling to emptiness. If you can remain unmoved by appearances while right in the midst of appearances, and not cling to emptiness while in the midst of emptiness, then inside and out nothing will confuse you. If you understand this teaching, you will gain awakening in an instant. "The Buddha's knowledge and vision" is simply this.

"Buddha" means awakened. Awakening could be divided into four aspects: one, initiating the Buddha's knowledge and vision; two, demonstrating the Buddha's knowledge and vision; three, fathoming the Buddha's knowledge and vision; and four, becoming one with the Buddha's knowledge and vision. If you investigate the initiating and demonstrating of the Buddha's knowledge and vision, you can easily fathom and become one with it. The 'Buddha's knowledge and vision' is just your fundamental true nature becoming manifest.

Be careful not to misconstrue the sutra's intent by supposing that the "initiating," "demonstrating," "fathoming," and "becoming" it describes is the Buddha's knowledge and vision, a knowledge and vision that we do not share in. If you interpret it in this way, you discredit the sutra and demean the Buddha. Since the Buddha is already awakened, perfect in knowledge and vision, why would there be any need for him to do it again?! You should now believe that the knowledge and vision of the Buddha is just your own mind; there is no other Buddha.

It is only because living beings cover over their own light with lust and craving for sensory experiences, become enslaved to things outside and disturbed within, that the World Honored One is roused from his samadhi to exhort them to cease, to not seek outside themselves, and instead to realize they are the same as the Buddha. Thus, the [Sutra] speaks of "realizing the Buddha's knowledge and vision."

I, too, am always exhorting people to realize the Buddha's knowledge and vision within their own minds. But ordinary people are perverse; confused and deluded, they do wrong. Their talk may be good, but their minds are bad. Greedy, hateful, envious, fawning and flattering, deceitful, and arrogant, they take advantage of others and harm living creatures. Thus, they only realize the knowledge and vision of living beings.

If you can constantly true your mind, activate your wisdom, observe and illuminate your own mind, refrain from evil while doing all that's good—this is you, yourself "realizing the knowledge and vision of the Buddha." In every moment of thought "realize the Buddha's knowledge and vision"; don't realize the knowledge and vision of living beings. Realizing the "Buddha's knowledge and vision" is to rise above the worldly; realizing the knowledge and vision of living beings is mundane. If you simply labor away reciting [the Sutra], and cling to it as an achievement, how is that any different from the yak fondly admiring its own tail?

Fada said, "Does that mean I shouldn't bother to recite the Sutra as long as I understand its meaning?" The Master replied:

How could the Sutra impede your mindfulness? Confusion and enlightenment are in the person; harm and benefit depend on you. If your mouth recites and your mind practices, you "turn" the Sutra; but if your mouth recites while your mind does not practice, then the Sutra "turns" you. Listen to my verse:

When your mind is confused, you are "turned" by the Dharma Flower;
When your mind is awakened, you turn the Dharma Flower.
Reciting the Sutra so long without understanding,
Has made you an enemy of its meaning.
To recite free of thoughts is correct,
With thoughts, your reciting goes wrong.
When both "with" or "without" are gone,
You may ride forever in the White Ox Cart.

Hearing this verse, Fada, wept spontaneously; the words moved him to an awakening. He told the Master, "All these years until today I have never actually 'turned' the *Dharma Flower [Lotus Sutra]*; instead I was turned by it."

Fada further said, "The Sutra says, 'Even if all the sravakas and bodhisattva disciples of the Buddha were to exhaust their minds trying to comprehend the Buddha's wisdom, they could never fathom it.' Now you would have ordinary people simply understand their own minds and call that 'the knowledge and vision of the Buddha.' Won't this cause those lacking superior faculties to doubt and revile the Sutra? Also, the Sutra speaks of three carts, drawn by a sheep, a deer, and an ox, as well as the White Ox Cart. How are these different? Please, explain these once again."

The Master said:

The Sutra's meaning is clear; you are the one who is confused. All the people of the three vehicles cannot fathom the Buddha's wisdom; the fault lies in their thinking. The more they think, the further away they go. The Buddha originally taught this principle for ordinary people, not for Buddhas. Those who were unable to believe were free to leave the assembly. They were unaware that they were sitting on the White Ox Cart; instead they went outside seeking the three vehicles. How much more clearly could the Sutra say it: "There is only one vehicle, Buddhahood; no other vehicle." Whether there might be two or three, and all the other countless provisional expedients, with the various stories, parables, and sayings—all these teachings are meant to lead to the One Buddha Vehicle. How can you not understand?! The three carts are provisional, an early and preliminary teaching. The one vehicle is real; meant for here and now. He is only teaching you to leave the provisional and return to the real. Once you return to the true and real, it too has no name.

You should understand that all the treasure and wealth comes from you; the carts' "use" depends on you. Don't keep thinking anymore of a "father," the "children," or the carts' "use." Not ruminating over this is called "holding-in-mind *The Lotus Sutra*." Then throughout all time your hands will never drop the Sutra; from morning to night it is always in your mind.

When Fada received this teaching, he was overwhelmed with joy, and recited a verse:

> *Three thousand recitations of the Sutra*
> *Are forgotten with one word from Caoxi [Huineng]*
> *Not grasping the transcendent meaning,*
> *How could I ever stop lifetimes of madness?*

> *Sheep, deer, and ox are just expedient devices, to*
> *Skillfully lay out beginning, midway, and end.*
> *Who could have imagined that within the burning house*
> *Sat the Dharma King all along?*

The Master said, "From now on you may be called 'the sutra-reciting monk.'"

From then on, although he understood the profound meaning, Fada continued to recite the Sutra unceasingly.

BHIKSHU ZHITONG

The monk Zhitong was a native of Anfeng in Shou Province. He had read *The Lankavatara Sutra* over a thousand times, but still did not understand the "three bodies," and the "four wisdoms." He bowed to the Master seeking an explanation of their meaning.

The Master said:

> As to the three bodies: the pure Dharma-body [Skt. *Dharmakaya*] is just your nature; the perfected Reward-body [Skt. *Sambhogakaya*] is your wisdom; and the thousands of millions of Transformed-bodies [Skt. *Nirmanakayas*] are what you do. If you describe the three bodies as something apart from your original nature, you have disembodied wisdom. If you realize that the three embodiments do not exist independently from your nature, you will then understand the four wisdoms of Bodhi. Listen to my verse:
>
> *Our own nature is complete with the Three Bodies;*
> *Understand this, and you gain the Four Wisdoms;*
> *You do not need to leave the realm of the senses*
> *To leap over into the Buddha's realm.*
>
> *Now I have explained this for you:*
> *Trust to this, and you'll never be confused,*
> *Like those who run outside in a frantic search for it,*
> *And spend their days talking about "bodhi."*

Zhitong asked further, "May I hear about the meaning of the four wisdoms?"

The Master replied:

Once you understand the three bodies, you understand the four wisdoms—why do you still ask about them? Talking about the four wisdoms as if they were something separate from the three bodies is to disembody wisdom. In this case, the wisdoms turn out to be no wisdom whatsoever.

He then gave this verse:

The wisdom of the great, perfect mirror,
Is your own nature, pure and clear.
The wisdom that sees the identical nature of all things,
Is your mind without defect;
Subtle, wondrous observing wisdom sees all effortlessly;
And the wisdom of doing-everything-successfully is like a spotless
*   mirror.*

Five and the eight together; sixth and seventh too—
Change and turn through cause and result.
Merely useful names; they have no real nature of their own.
If in the place of change and turning, you don't linger on feelings;
You flourish and forever abide in the samadhi of the dragon.

Gloss: *Thus are the consciousnesses transformed into the wisdoms. In the teachings it says, "The first five consciousnesses when turned become 'wisdom of doing-everything-successfully'; the sixth consciousness when turned becomes 'subtle, wondrous observing wisdom'; the seventh consciousness when turned becomes the 'wisdom that sees the identical nature of all things'; and, the eighth consciousness when turned becomes the 'wisdom of the great, perfect mirror.'" Although the sixth and seventh are turned within the causal sphere, and the fifth and eighth in*

74

the realms of effects, these are changes in name only; the consciousness themselves are not transformed in their essence.[37]

Zhitong suddenly realized the essential nature of the wisdoms and presented a verse of his own:

> *The three bodies are my basic being;*
> *Four wisdoms, my own clear, bright mind.*
> *With bodies and wisdoms in unobstructed fusion,*
> *I can respond to beings, and accord in kind;*
> *To consciously cultivate them is in vain;*
> *Holding to or pondering them is wasted effort;*
> *The Master now made the subtle meaning clear to me:*
> *And in the end I lose the stain of names.*

BHIKSHU ZHICHANG

The monk Zhichang was from Guixi in Xin Province. He left home to become a monk when he was a child and was intent on discovering his own nature. One day he visited the Master, and paid his respects.

The Master asked him, "Where are you from, and what do you want?"

He replied, "I recently went to White Peak Mountain [Baifeng Shan] in Hong Province where I bowed in respect to High Master Datong to receive his instruction on realizing Buddhahood by seeing one's nature. But I have some lingering doubts, so I have traveled this great distance to bow to you. I humbly hope that the Master will be so compassionate to guide me."

The Master said, "What did he teach you? Try to repeat his actual words to me."

---

37 The above interlinear commentarial explanation of this difficult verse was not part of the original text, but was added later.

Zhichang said, "I was there for three months without having received any instructions. Being eager for the Dharma, one evening I went alone to the abbot's room and asked him, 'What is my original mind, my fundamental nature?'

"Datong then said to me, 'Do you see empty space?' 'Yes,' I answered, 'I see it.' Datong said, 'When you see empty space, what appearance does it have?' I replied, 'Empty space is formless. How could it have an appearance?!' Datong said, 'Your fundamental nature is just like empty space in that there is not a single thing that can be seen. This is called, *true seeing*. And there's nothing that can be known—this is called *true knowing*. It has no blue or yellow, long or short. Just seeing the purity of the original source, that the essence of enlightenment is perfect and bright—this is called "realizing Buddhahood by seeing one's nature." It is also called, "the knowledge and vision of the Tathagata."' Although I heard this explanation, I still do not understand, and implore you, Master, instruct me."

The Master said:

> That teacher's explanation still retains the idea of knowing and seeing; that's why you haven't fully understood. Now I will teach you through a verse:
>
> *Not to see a single thing, still holds on to seeing "nothing,"*
> *Much like floating clouds blocking the face of the sun.*
> *Not to know a single thing, still holds to knowing "nothing,"*
> *Even as lightning flashes out of empty space.*
>
> *If this kind of "not-knowing, not-seeing" arises even for an instant;*
> *You lack discernment—so how could you ever figure out expedients?*
> *If you can immediately realize your error,*
> *Your own spiritual light will always shine forth.*

When Zhichang heard this verse, [the truth of it] suddenly dawned on him in both heart and mind. He then composed this verse:

Pointlessly setting up notions of knowing and seeing,
I sought for Bodhi, attached to appearances;
Clinging to even one thought of enlightenment,
How could I rise above my previous confusion?

Our own nature is the essential source of awakening,
And can navigate the turning, twisting flow;
Had I not entered the Patriarch's room,
I'd still be drifting between the two extremes.

One day Zhichang asked the Master, "The Buddha expounded the teachings of the three vehicles, yet he also spoke of the highest vehicle. Your disciple still doesn't quite understand this. Could you explain it for me?"

The Master said:

Only pay attention to your own original mind; don't get entangled in the external form of the Dharma. The Dharma does not have four different vehicles; it is peoples' minds that differ. Learning through reading, listening, and reciting is the small vehicle. Awakening to dharmas and understanding their meaning is the middle vehicle. Cultivating according to the teachings is the great vehicle. To completely fathom the ten thousand things all the while remaining undefiled by anything, detached from appearances, not grasping anything at all—this is the highest vehicle. Vehicles are methods of practice; not subjects for debate. Cultivate yourself; don't ask me. At all times, your own essential nature is itself "truly as it is."

Zhichang bowed in gratitude, and served the master for the rest of his life.

BHIKSHU ZHIDAO

The bhikshu Zhidao was a native of Nanhai in Guang Province. He asked the Master to help him, "Since leaving home to become a monk, I have spent more than ten years studying *The Nirvana Sutra*, but still haven't grasped its deep meaning. Please, Master, help me to understand."

The Master said, "On which point are you unclear?"

Zhidao answered, "'All events and activities are impermanent; they arise and perish. When the arising and perishing itself ceases, that very ceasing is bliss.' I have doubts about this passage."

The Master said, "What are your doubts?"

Zhidao replied, "All living beings have two bodies, the physical body and the Dharma-body. The physical body is impermanent, it is born and dies. The Dharma-body is permanent and has no awareness or consciousness. The Sutra says that the very ceasing of birth and death, arising and perishing, is bliss. But I wonder: which body ceases, and which enjoys the bliss? When the physical body perishes, the four elements scatter.[38] That is total suffering; such misery cannot be called bliss! If it's the Dharma-body that ceases, it would be just like grass and trees, rocks and stones—who is there to experience bliss?

"Moreover, the Dharma-nature is the essence, and the five skandhas are the functioning of birth and death. One essence has five functions. So birth and death are permanent, eternal: because birth initiates the functions that go forth from the essence, and at death the functions withdraw and revert back into the essence. If there is rebirth, then sentient beings never cease to exist and never die. If, on the other hand, there is no rebirth, then sentient beings would simply die out and be forever extinct, the same as inanimate things.

38 An allusion to the physical body (Skt. *rupa*), that which has mass, occupies space, and consisting of the four great elements: earth, air, fire, and water.

Thus all things would stop with nirvana—and since one does not even get to live, how could there be bliss?"

The Master said:

You are a disciple of the Buddha! How can you use the perverse and heretical views of nihilism and eternalism to discuss the supreme vehicle teachings?! According to what you say, there is a separate Dharma-body outside the physical body; and that one must transcend birth and death in order to seek for "still cessation" [nirvana]. Also, you suppose the eternal bliss of nirvana is a physical experience. All of this is just attaching to birth and death, and obsessing on worldly pleasure.

You should know that the Buddha [taught] because deluded people mistook the combination of the five skandhas for their own essence and being, and discriminated so as to make all things external to themselves. They loved life and dreaded death, drifted and flowed along from thought to thought, unaware that this was all an unreal dream, hollow and false. They pointlessly turned round and round on the wheel of birth and death, wrongly imagining that the eternal bliss of nirvana was some kind of suffering, and all day long frantically sought after something else. Taking pity on them, the Buddha pointed out the true bliss of nirvana: if even for an instant there is no sign of arising and no sign of passing, then there is no birth and death to be ended, and right there is to enjoy "still cessation." But when it is right there, if one has no thought of it being right there, this is permanence and bliss. This bliss is neither "enjoyed" nor "not enjoyed." How can you call this "one essence with five functions?!" Worse, how can you go on to say that "nirvana stops everything" forever? This is to demean the Buddha and disparage the Dharma. Listen to my verse:

Unsurpassable, great nirvana:
Perfect, bright, always serene and illuminating.
Confused people call it death;
Outside-the-Way believers imagine it as "nothingness."
Seekers of the two vehicles
Think it is "doing nothing."
All these arise from emotions and longings:
The root of the sixty-two wrong views.
They arbitrarily create empty names, but
Do they have any real meaning?

Only those who go beyond conjecture,
Free from grasping or rejecting,
Can penetrate the teaching of the five skandhas, and
The "self" the skandhas uphold.
The external appearances of things—
The mass of forms,
Each and every sound,
Are all alike: dreams and illusions.

For them, ideas of "sacred" and "worldly" never occur;
Nor do they expound upon nirvana,
The two boundaries of emptiness and existence,
And three times—they go beyond them all;
Their senses active, functioning, responding,
Yet they never need to ponder things over.
Discerning all things, clearly distinguishing,
Yet free of any thought of discrimination.

When the aeon-ending fires burn to the bottom of the sea,
And the winds pound the mountains like drums,

The true bliss of permanent quiescence—
The mark of nirvana remains, as it really is.

I am forcing these words now,
To get you to give up your wrong views.
Don't try to understand by following my words,
And then you may indeed understand it a bit.

Hearing this verse, Zhidao experienced a profound awakening. Overjoyed, he bowed and withdrew.

CHAN MASTER XINGSI

Chan Master Xingsi was born to the Liu family of Ancheng in Ji Province. Hearing about the flourishing influence of the Caoxi teaching, he went directly to visit and pay his respects. He asked, "How can someone avoid falling into the gradual stage-by-stage way of practice?"

The Master said, "What were you practicing before coming here?" He replied, "I didn't even work on the Four Noble Truths." The Master said, "Then what stage could you fall into?" He then said, "If one isn't practicing the Four Truths, could there be any stages?" The Master was deeply impressed with Xingsi and made him head of the assembly.

One day, the Master said to him, "You should go now and teach elsewhere; never let the teaching die out." Having realized the Dharma, Xingsi returned to Green Mountain Highlands [Qingyuan Mountain] in Ji province where he spread the teaching and influenced many to change. (After his death he was given the posthumous title Chan Master Vastly Liberating Hongji).

CHAN MASTER HUAIRANG

Chan Master Huairang was a son of the Du family in Jin Province. First he studied under National Master An of Song Mountain, who told him to go to Caoxi and pursue his studies. When he arrived, he bowed, and the Master asked him, "What has come?" He answered, "Song Mountain." The Master said, "What is this thing, and why does it come?" He replied, "To say it is like a thing, misses the point." The Master said, "Then what is there to be cultivated and certified?" He replied, "Cultivation and certification cannot be absent, but defilement cannot be present."

The Master said, "Just this being free of any defilement is what all Buddhas guard and maintain. You are like this; and I am like this too. In India [the 'West' in relation to China] Prajnatara prophesized: 'A galloping colt will come from beneath your feet who will leave in his dust everyone else in the world.' Keep this in mind, but don't speak of it too soon." *(Another version did not include the above prophecy beginning with 'In India . . .')*

Huairang immediately understood, and accordingly he stayed on for fifteen years as the Master's attendant; day by day becoming more immersed in the deep and the profound. He later went to Nanyue where he extensively spread the Chan tradition. (He was posthumously given the title, Chan Master Deep Insight—Dahui).

CHAN MASTER XUANJUE

Chan Master Xuanjue of Yongjia was from the Dai family of Wen Province. When he was young, he studied the sutras and commentaries and was well-versed in the Tiantai Dharma practice of "calming and contemplating." Upon reading *The Vimalakirti Sutra*, he understood the mind-ground.

One day he happened to meet the Master's disciple, Xuance, and they had an engaging discussion. Everything Xuanjue said implicitly accorded with the teachings of all the Patriarchs. Xuance asked him, "Kind Sir, who did you receive this teaching from?"

Xuanjue replied, "I heard the various Mahayana sutra and shastra texts each from different masters, and later when I read *The Vimalakirti Sutra*, I awakened to the source of the Buddha-mind. As yet, however, no one has certified my realization."

Xuance said, "That self-certification was acceptable before the time of the first Buddha, King with an Awesome Voice, but after him, all who 'self-enlighten' without a teacher risk falling into a misguided naturalism, an Outside-the-Way notion."

Xuanjue asked, "Then will you please certify me, Kind Sir?" Xuance replied, "My words carry no weight, but in Caoxi there is a High Master, the Sixth Patriarch. Students gather there from all over, like clouds, to receive teaching from one who has the Dharma. If you want to go, I will accompany you."

Xuanjue then went with Xuance to call on the Master. On arriving, Xuanjue circumambulated the Master three times, shook his ringed staff, and stood there boldly in front of him. The Master said, "A sramana [renunciant monk] carries himself perfectly, guided by the three thousand forms of deportment and the eighty thousand subtle ways of behavior, where do you come from, 'Great Worthy One,' that makes you so conceited?!"

Xuanjue said, "Birth and death are a grave matter; impermanence comes swiftly."

The Master replied, "Why don't you seize the essence of it: that there is no birth, and no 'swift,' either?"

He replied, "The essence is birthless, and understanding basically has no speed."

The Master said, "So it is. So it is."

Xuanjue only then bowed with full and perfect deportment. A short while later, he announced that he was leaving, and the Master said,

"Aren't you leaving rather quickly?"

He answered, "Fundamentally I don't move; so how could I be quick?"

The Master said, "Who knows you don't move?"

He replied, "Kind Sir, you are making this discrimination yourself."

The Master said, "You truly understand the meaning of the birthless."

Xuanjue asked, "How can the birthless have a 'meaning'?"

"If it has no meaning to it, then who makes this discrimination?" the Master asked.

Xuanjue replied, "Discrimination itself has no meaning either."

The Master exclaimed, "Excellent! Please at least stay for the night."

From then on he was known as "the Overnight Awakened One." Later he wrote *The Song of Awakening*, which circulated widely. (His posthumous title became Wuxiang—Great Master Beyond Knowing—and in his time he was known as Truly Awakened—Zhenjue.)

CHAN MASTER ZHIHUANG

Chan practitioner Zhihuang first studied under the Fifth Patriarch. Thinking he had already realized genuine samadhi, he lived in a hut and devoted himself to constant sitting meditation for twenty years. When the Master's disciple Xuance was wandering through the Heshuo area, he heard of Zhihuang's reputation and paid a visit to his hut.

There he asked him, "What are you doing here?"

"Entering concentration," replied Zhihuang.

Xuance said, "You say you are 'entering concentration'; do you have a thought of entering, or are you entering without thought? If you enter without thought, then all insentient things like grass and trees, rocks and stones, should attain 'samadhi.' If you enter with thought, then all sentient beings with consciousness should attain samadhi."

Zhihuang said, "When I properly enter samadhi, I don't notice whether I am thinking or not."

Xuance said, "Not noticing whether or not you are engaged in thought is permanent concentration. So how can you enter or come out of that? If you enter and come out of it, it is not the great concentration."

Zhihuang was speechless. After a long while, he finally asked, "Who is your teacher?"

Xuance said, "My master is the Sixth Patriarch at Caoxi."

Zhihuang said, "What does the Sixth Patriarch take chan[39] concentration to be?"

Xuance replied, "My teacher explains it as a subtle, wondrous, perfect serenity that interacts both in essence and application with reality as it truly is. Here, the five skandhas are fundamentally empty; the six sensory realms do not exist. One neither enters or comes out of this samadhi concentration; it cannot be settled-into or disturbed. The essence of chan concentration is non-dwelling, clinging to nothing; it goes beyond even the act of 'dwelling' in meditative stillness. Chan concentration by its very nature cannot be initiated, and you cannot even conceive the thought or idea of it. The mind is like empty space, yet without even a notion of empty space."

Hearing this explanation, Zhihuang went directly to see the Master. The Master asked him, "Kind Sir, where are you from?" And Zhihuang related the previous exchange in full.

The Master then said, "It is truly as you were told. Simply let your mind be like empty space, without attaching to an idea of your mind

---

39 Chan/chan. Upper-case "C" is used when referring to a particular school, or Dharma Master with the title "Chan Master." Lower-case "c" is used when referring generically to the various methods of dhyana meditation exercises, as in "sitting chan."

as empty space; responding appropriately without any hindrance, clear-of-mind whether moving or still. Distinctions like 'worldly' and 'holy,' forgotten; subject and object, dissolved. Essence and appearance are 'just so; as they really are,'—then there is no time you are not in chan concentration." *(Another version does not include the above passage beginning with 'simply let your mind . . .' It merely says, 'The Master took pity on him because he came from far away, so he taught him, clearing up his doubts').*

At this Zhihuang experienced a profound awakening. All that he had attained in twenty years vanished from his mind without a trace. That night the people of Hebei heard a voice in space announcing, "Today, Chan master Zhihuang realized the Way."

Later, Zhihuang bowed and left, returning to Hebei where he taught the monks, nuns, laywomen and laymen.

ONE MEMBER OF THE SANGHA

A sangha member asked the Master, "What kind of person gets the 'essence of meaning' from Huangmei?"

The Master replied, "Someone who understands the Buddhadharma."

The sanghan asked, "High Master, did you get it?"

The Master replied, "I do not understand the Buddhadharma."

BHIKSHU FANGBIAN

One day the Master wanted to wash the robe that had been handed down to him, but there was no good spring nearby, so he went a few miles behind the monastery where he saw a lush mountain forest vibrant with auspicious energy. He shook his ringed staff, and then stuck it into the ground, and a spring bubbled forth to form a pool. As the Master was kneeling to wash his robe on a rock, a monk suddenly appeared on the rocks, and bowed to him, and said, "I am Fangbian, from Western Shu [Sichuan]. Some time ago I was in southern India, where I visited the Great Master Bodhidharma. He told me, 'Go to China right away; the true Treasure of Genuine-Dharma-Discernment and the robe I inherited from Mahakashyapa has been bequeathed to the sixth generation at Caoxi in Shao Province. Go there and pay your respects.' I have come a long way; please show me the robe and bowl you have inherited."

The Master showed them to him, and asked, "Noble One, what kind of work do you do?" "I am a skilled sculptor," he replied. Keeping a straight face, the Master said, "Then try sculpting me." Fangbian was at a loss, but after several days he completed a lifelike image of the Patriarch, seven inches tall, wonderful in every detail. The Master laughed, saying, "You only understand the nature of image-making; you do not understand the buddha-nature." Then the Master reached out his hand and rubbed the crown of Fangbian's head, saying, "Long will you be a field of blessings for people and gods."

(The Master rewarded him with a robe. Fangbian divided it into three sections: one he used to wrap the sculpture; another he kept for himself; and the third he wrapped in palm leaves and buried in the ground. He vowed, "In the future, I will appear in the world, recover this robe, and I will on this spot restore the monastery where I will then reside as its abbot." In the eighth year of the Jiayou period of the Song dynasty, [1063], a monk by the name of Weixin built a monastic hall on this site. When he dug into the ground, he discovered the robe, which was still in new condition. The sculpture Fangbian made of the Master is at Gaoquan si, [High Springs Monastery]; those who venerate it often experience a response.)

MASTER WOLUN'S VERSE

A member of the sangha was reciting Master Wolun's verse:

Wolun has the skill to
Stop the hundred thoughts;
Facing situations, his mind does not respond;
Bodhi increases day by day.

When the Master heard this, he said, "This verse [author] does not understand the mind-ground; if you cultivate by it, you will only increase your bondage." He then gave this verse:

Huineng has no skill, to
Stop the hundred thoughts.
Facing situations, his mind often responds;
How could Bodhi increase?

CHAPTER EIGHT

Direct and Gradual

While the Patriarch was living at Baolin [Jewel-Wood Monastery] in Caoxi, the Venerable Master Shenxiu resided at Jade Spring [Yuquan] Monastery in Jingnan. Both teachers' schools flourished in their time, and everyone called them "Southern Neng" and "Northern Xiu." So it was that there came a division into two schools, "northern" and "southern," "direct" and "gradual." Their students, however, did not understand the meaning of this distinction.

The Master said to the assembly,

> The Dharma is originally a single school; it is people who think 'north' and 'south.' The Dharma is of one kind; but the understanding of it may be 'direct' or 'gradual.' So why the terms 'direct' and 'gradual'? Dharma itself is neither 'direct' nor 'gradual.' Rather it is people who are sharp or dull. Hence the terms 'direct' and 'gradual.'

The followers of Shenxiu, nevertheless, often criticized the southern Patriarch for being illiterate, and questioned his achievement. But Shenxiu himself said, "He has reached awakening without the benefit of a teacher and deeply understands the supreme vehicle; I am not his equal. Furthermore, my Master, the Fifth Patriarch, personally bequeathed the robe and teaching to him—how could that have been in error? I regret that I cannot make the long journey to be close to him, yet I receive state patronage without deserving it. You should not linger here; go to Caoxi and resolve your doubts."

One day Shenxiu instructed his close disciple, Zhicheng, "You are bright and very knowledgeable; go to Caoxi for me and listen to his teaching. Remember and record everything you hear, so you can tell me all of it when you come back."

As ordered, Zhicheng went to Caoxi; there he joined the assembly without saying where he had come from. At that time, the Patriarch announced to the assembly, "Today there is a thief hiding among you who has come to steal the teaching." Zhicheng immediately stepped forward, bowed, and told the whole story behind his mission. The Master said, "You are from Jade Spring; you must be a spy." "Not so," he replied. The Master asked, "How can you not be?" He answered, "Before I confessed, I was; but now that I have admitted to it, I am not."

The Master asked, "How does your Master instruct his followers?" Zhicheng replied, "He always instructs his students to stop the mind and contemplate stillness; and to sit upright at all times without lying down."

The Master said:

> To stop the mind and contemplate stillness is a sickness, not chan meditation. Constant sitting restricts the body—how could it help towards [discovering] truth? Listen to my verse:
>
> *You can sit without lying down from the moment you're born,*
> *But when you die, you'll lie down, never again to sit.*
> *How could you build a solid practice*
> *On a set of stinking bones?!*

Zhicheng bowed again and said, "This disciple studied the Way for nine years with Master Shenxiu without realizing any awakening. Now, hearing a single explanation from the High Master, I am reunited with my original mind. For me, the matter of birth and death is a serious concern. Would the Master please be compassionate and teach me more?"

The Master said, "I have heard that your master teaches students about morality, concentration, and wisdom. Please tell me, how does he say to practice them?" Zhicheng replied, "Great Master, Shenxiu says, 'doing no evil' is morality; that 'doing good' is wisdom; and, that purifying one's own mind is concentration. This is how he explains them. I wonder, High Master, what teaching do you give?"

The Master said, "If I said I had a teaching to give others, I would be deceiving you. Depending on the situation, I merely use expedients to untie people's bonds, and provisionally call it 'samadhi.' Your master's explanations of morality, concentration, and wisdom are truly wonderful; I see morality, concentration, and wisdom somewhat differently." Zhicheng said, "There can only be one kind of morality, concentration, and wisdom. How can there be a difference?"

The Master said:

> Your master's morality, concentration, and wisdom are meant for Great Vehicle practitioners; my morality, concentration, and wisdom are meant for those of the Supreme Vehicle. Awakening and understanding are not the same; seeing may come slowly or immediately. Listen to my explanation, and see if it's the same as his.
>
> My teaching never departs from the essential nature; to depart from the essential nature in explaining the Dharma is teaching superficially, and this only leads to confusion. You should realize that the ten thousand dharmas all flow from our own essential nature. This is the true teaching of morality, concentration, and wisdom. Listen to my verse:
>
> > *Mind-ground free from error: essential nature's morality.*
> > *Mind-ground free from delusion: essential nature's wisdom.*
> > *Mind-ground undisturbed: essential nature's concentration.*
> > *It never increases or decreases: indestructible as vajra.*
> > *The body comes and goes, [yet] you're rooted in samadhi.*

Hearing this verse, Zhicheng apologized, and in gratitude offered a verse of his own:

The five heaps [Skt. skandhas], an illusory body—
And how could an illusion be ultimate?
Even wanting to reach the 'truly so'
Means the method is not yet pure.

The Master approved, and further said to Zhicheng:

Your master's morality, concentration, and wisdom exhorts those with lesser capacities for wisdom; my morality, concentration, and wisdom motivates those with a greater capacity for wisdom. If you awaken to your essential nature, you do not set up [ideas of] "bodhi" or "nirvana," or "liberated knowing and seeing." Only when you understand there is nothing to attain, can you set up all the myriad teachings. If you understand this, you are "embodying the Buddha"; it is also called "bodhi" and "nirvana," and "liberated knowing and seeing." Those who see their essential nature can set these up or not as they choose. They can come and go freely, unhindered and spontaneous. Everything they do and all their words are appropriate, timely, and according to need. Wherever and however they appear, they never depart from the inherent nature. They are just "realizing the spiritual powers of self-mastery," and "the samadhi of playfulness." This is called "seeing the nature."

Zhicheng further asked the Master, "What is the meaning of 'not setting up'?"

The Master replied:

When your essential nature is free from error, unobstructed, un-disturbed and unconfused, when prajna oversees and illuminates your every thought, and you are far removed from the superficial appearances of things, independent and free absolutely everywhere and anywhere—what is there to "set up?"

Awaken by yourself to your own essential nature; awaken directly by cultivating directly. There are no gradual stages; nor anything to set up. All things are "still and empty"—how could they be arranged in a sequence?

Zhicheng bowed, and vowed to attend on the Master morning and night without fail. (Cheng came from Taihe in Ji province).

BHIKSHU ZHICHE

The monk Zhiche was from Jiangxi. His family name was Zhang, and his given name was Xingchang. In his youth he had been a wandering martial artist. Ever since the division into the Southern and Northern schools, although the two leaders had lost any sense of "self and other," their followers were fiercely competitive and partisan. Resenting the public's knowledge of the Patriarch's having received the robe, the disciples of the Northern school set up Master Shenxiu as their own Sixth Patriarch. Then they hired Xingchang to assassinate the Master.

But the Master had the ability to know the thoughts of others and in advance, placed ten ounces of gold by his chair. That night, Xingchang slipped into the Master's room to kill him. The Master stretched out his neck to the sword. Xingchang slashed with his blade three times, but could not injure him.

The Master said:

> A straight sword will not be bent;
> A crooked sword cannot [cut] straight.
> I merely owe you gold, not my life.

Xingchang fell to the ground in shock. After quite a while he came to his senses and begged for forgiveness, repenting of his error. Then he wanted to leave home and become a monk. The Master gave him the gold, and said, "You must go. I fear my followers may harm you out of revenge. Change your appearance and come back someday; then I will accept you."

Xingchang did as he was instructed and vanished into the night. Later he became a monk, took full ordination, and vigorously trained himself. One day, remembering what the Master had said, he made the long journey back to pay his respects.

The Master said, "I have been thinking about you for a long time; what took you so long?" Xingchang replied, "Previously the Master forgave my crime. Although I have become a monk and practice asceticism, I could never repay your kindness. If only I could spread the Dharma and liberate living beings! Your disciple constantly studies *The Mahaparinirvana Sutra*, but still does not understand the meanings of 'permanence' and 'impermanence.' Will the High Master please be compassionate and explain them for me?"

The Master said, "Impermanence is just the buddha-nature; and what is permanent is just the discriminating mind with all its good and bad states."

Xingchang replied, "Your explanation contradicts the Sutra text!" The Master said, "I transmit the authentic mind-seal of the Buddha. How could what I say contradict the Buddha's sutras?" Xingchang answered, "The Sutra says that the buddha-nature is permanent; but you say it is impermanent. It says that good and bad dharmas, even the aspiration for bodhi, are impermanent, but the Master says they are permanent. These contradictions have made me even more confused."

The Master said, "In the past I heard the bhikshuni [nun] Wujinzang [Inexhaustible Treasure] reciting *The Nirvana Sutra*, and then explained it for her with not so much as a single word or meaning out of accord with the Sutra. My explanation to you now is exactly the same." Xingchang replied, "Your student's capacity for understanding is shallow. Please High Master, explain this for me in more detail."

The Master said:

Don't you realize—if the buddha-nature were permanent, then what good or bad states would there be to speak of? And not a single person until the end of time would ever aspire to bodhi. That is why I say it is impermanent. This is precisely the path to true permanence taught by the Buddha. Moreover, if all things were impermanent, then everything would have its own nature which was subject to birth and death, and the truly permanent nature would not be universal, all-pervading. That is why I say they are permanent. And that is precisely what the Buddha meant by teaching true impermanence.

Ordinary people and seekers outside-the-Way, cling to misguided ideas of permanence. While those who follow the path of the two vehicles, mistake what is permanent as impermanent, and then from this formulate eight wrong views. Because of this, the Buddha gave the complete teaching of *The Nirvana Sutra* to refute these biased views and clearly explain true permanence, true bliss, true self, and true purity. You are now overly dependent on the words and missing the meaning. You thus end up misunderstanding the Buddha's sublime, complete final statement as if it meant a nihilistic impermanence or a lifeless permanence. Even if you read the Sutra a thousand times, what benefit would you get from it?

Xingchang suddenly experienced a great awakening; after which he gave this verse:

For those who clung to impermanence,
The Buddha taught there is permanence.
Not understanding how expedients work,
I was just picking up pebbles from a spring pond.
But now without expending any effort,
The buddha-nature appears right before me.
The Master did not bestow it,
And I did not obtain a single thing.

The Master said, "Now you understand! You should be called Zhiche [Intent on Knowing]."

Zhiche bowed in gratitude, and withdrew.

BHIKSHU SHENHUI

There was a boy, age thirteen, named Shenhui, who was from the Gao family in Xiangyang. He came from Jade Spring [Yuquan] to pay his respects. The Master said, "Wise friend, you have come a long way; made a hard journey, but did you bring the 'original' with you? If you have the original, you should know the owner. Can you explain this to me?" Shenhui replied, "'Clinging to nothing' is the original; 'seeing' is the owner." The Master said, "What will this sramanera [novice monk] dare to say next?!" Shenhui then asked, "When you sit in chan meditation, High Master, do you see or not?" The Master hit him three times with his staff, and asked, "When I hit you, does it hurt or not?" He replied, "It both hurts and does not hurt." The Master said, "I both see and do not see." Shenhui asked, "How can you both see and not see?"

The Master replied:

> I constantly see the faults and errors of my own mind. I do not see the rights and wrongs, good or bad, of others. This is my seeing and not seeing. How can you say it both hurts and does not hurt? If it does not hurt, then you're as unfeeling as wood or stone. But if it does hurt, then you are just an ordinary person who gets angry and resentful. The seeing and not seeing you spoke of just now arc the two extremes, and you hurting yet not hurting are birth and death. You haven't even recognized your own nature, yet you boldly play around with others.

Shenhui bowed, and apologized. He thanked the Master. The Master continued:

> If your mind is confused and you do not see, then ask a Good and Wise Advisor to show you the path. If your mind is awakened, then you see your own nature, and so cultivate according to the teaching. You yourself are confused, and do not see your own mind; yet you come asking me if I see or not. If I see, I know it myself—how could that be of any help to you in your confusion? Similarly, if you yourself see, it won't get rid of my confusion. So why don't you see and know for yourself, instead of asking me whether or not I see?

Shenhui bowed again, over one hundred times, seeking to be forgiven for his error. He served the master diligently, never leaving his side.

One day the Master said to the community, "I have something with no head or tail, no name, no label, no back or front. Do you know what it is?" Shenhui stepped forward and said, "It is the root and source of all Buddhas; my buddha-nature!" The Master said, "I just told you that it had no name or label, and you immediately go and call it 'the root source of all Buddhas.' Go and build a thatched hut over your head. You are just an intellectual pretending to know."

After the Master passed away, Shenhui went to Jingluo [the former capital] where he propagated the direct teaching of Caoxi. He wrote a treatise, "Notes Revealing the Source," which circulated widely in his time. (He became known as Chan Master He ze.)

THE CRITICS

The Master noticed that many critics from various schools and sects, all ill-intentioned, had gathered beneath his seat. Pitying them, he said, "Students of the Way, get rid of all thoughts of good and bad. What cannot be named by any name is the essential nature. The nature free of any duality can be called the real nature. It is on the basis of this true nature that all the teaching methods are established. At these words, you should see it for yourselves."

Hearing this, they all bowed and asked him to be their teacher.

CHAPTER NINE

Imperial Summons

On the fifteenth day of the first month, during the first year of Shenlong [Divine Dragon] reign [705 C.E.], the Empress Wu Zetian and the Emperor Zhongzong issued a proclamation of summons, as follows:

> We have invited the two masters, An and Xiu [Huian and Shenxiu] to the palace to accept our offerings, so that we can investigate the one vehicle in the leisure time remaining to us after fulfilling our myriad duties. Those two teachers have deferred, saying that in the South there is a Chan Master Huineng, who was personally bequeathed the robe and Dharma of the Great Master Hongren, and who now carries forward the mind-seal[40] of the Buddha; and that we should invite and inquire of him. We are now sending the court Chamberlain, Xuejian, with this invitation in the hope that the Master will regard us compassionately and swiftly come to the capital.

The Master formally declined on the grounds of illness, saying that he wished to spend his remaining days in the forest monastery.

Xuejian said, "The worthy chan masters at the capital all said that one must sit in chan meditation and practice concentration to gain

---

40 The term "mind-seal" (*xin yin* 心印) is a Buddhist metaphor derived from the tradition of an emperor or high authority using a red-inked stamp, or carved seal (*yin* 印), to authenticate important documents by pressing it on a piece of paper. The Buddha's mind-seal, however, is not a "thing" transmitted. Rather, it is an expression of recognition by the teacher that a disciple has through their own efforts realized the profound meaning of all Buddhas, and is ready to become an heir to and transmitter of this source-teaching. It implies that the awakened mind of the Buddha has been replicated directly, as it were, in the mind of the disciple.

an understanding of the Way; for without chan concentration, liberation is impossible. I wonder, what is your teaching?"

The Master said:

The Way is realized through the mind. How could it come from sitting? *The Diamond Sutra* says, "If you claim that the Tathagata either sits or lies down, you are traveling a wrong path. Why? Because he neither comes from anywhere, nor goes anywhere." Freedom from birth and death is the Tathagata's pure chan meditation. The still emptiness of all things is the Tathagata's pure chan sitting. Ultimately there is no realization; how much the less "sitting."

Xuejian said, "When I return to the palace, their majesties will surely question me. Please, Master, be so kind as to instruct me on the essentials of the mind, so that I can pass it along to the two rulers and students of the Way in the capital. It will be like one lamp lighting a hundred thousand lamps, light upon light without end illuminating the darkness."

The Master said:

The Way is beyond light or dark. Light and darkness are complementary ideas; they are relative terms, so even "endless light" must have an end. Therefore, *The Vimalakirti Sutra* says, "The Dharma has no comparison, because there is nothing relative in it."

Xuejian said, "Light symbolizes wisdom; darkness symbolizes the afflictions. If cultivators of the Way do not use wisdom to expose and untangle the afflictions, how can they liberate themselves from beginningless births and deaths?"

The Master said:

The afflictions themselves are bodhi; they are non-dual, correlated. Someone who uses wisdom to expose and eliminate the afflictions has the understanding of the two-vehicles, a teaching suitable for the sheep and deer carts. Those of the highest wisdom are not like this at all.

Xuejian asked, "What is the great vehicle view and understanding?" The Master answered:

Ordinary people see light and darkness as two different things, but the wise realize they are essentially non-dual. Our real nature is non-dual. It is not diminished in ordinary people, nor is it greater in worthy sages. It is not disturbed amid the afflictions; nor is it stilled and static while in chan concentration. It does not end, nor endure forever. It does not arrive or leave; and has no location: neither inside nor outside nor in the middle. Unborn, undying, its essence and appearance is "just so; as it really is." It is permanent and unchanging—it is called the "Way."

Xuejian said, "How is your explanation of 'unborn and undying,' different from outside-the-Way teachings?" The Master answered:

The unborn and undying of which the outside-ways speak depicts nothingness as the end to life, and life as the clear contrast to nothingness. Their nothingness is not really nothing; and the life of which they speak is not really life. In the unborn and undying I speak of originally there was no birth [then], nor is there any death now. Therefore, I teach something very different from them. If you wish to understand the essentials of the mind, simply do not deliberate over good and bad; and you will spontaneously access the pure essence of the mind, which is always still like deep, clear water, [yet] with subtle functions as numerous as sand grains in the Ganges River.

Hearing this explanation, Xuejian experienced an immediate and expansive awakening. He bowed, took his leave, and returned to the palace, where he reported the Master's words.

That year, on the third day of the ninth month, an imperial proclamation was issued extolling the Master:

> Due to old age and illness, the Master declined our invitation. Cultivating the Way for us, you are a field of blessings for the country, just like Vimalakirti who used his illness to expound the Mahayana in Vaisali. You pass along the mind of the Buddhas and expound the non-dual Dharma. Xuejian has conveyed the Master's teaching of the knowledge and vision of the Tathagata. Because of accumulated good deeds, and roots of goodness planted in previous lives, we are fortunate to be born at a time when the Master is in the world, and to directly awaken to the Supreme Vehicle. We bow our heads in unending gratitude for your kindness.
>
> The Master is also presented with a fine formal robe and a crystal bowl as gifts, and the governor of Shao Province is commanded to restore and refurbish the monastery buildings. The Master's former residence is to be converted into a temple, called the Nation's Gratitude [Guoen] Monastery.

CHAPTER TEN

Final Instructions

One day the Master summoned his disciples Fahai, Zhicheng, Fada, Shenhui, Zhichang, Zhitong, Zhiche, Zhidao, Fazhen, and Faru, and said to them:

You are different from the others. After I pass away, you should each go and become a master in a different region. I will now teach you how to explain the Dharma without departing from its original source.

First, you should bring up the teaching of the three classifications of dharmas, and then the thirty-six complementary pairs—answer [any] with its opposite; this avoids [setting up in] either side.

In explaining all these teachings, never depart from the essential nature. If someone should suddenly ask about something, answer with its opposite, thus neutralizing the pair. Always find the opposite principle: for example, "coming" and "going" are relative to each other; ultimately the two cancel each other out—and then there is no place to set up.

The teaching of the three classifications of dharmas are the "heaps," "realms," and "entrances." The five "heaps" [Skt. *skandhas*] are: form, feelings, perception, mental "actions" and impulses, and consciousness. The twelve "entrances" [Skt. *ayatana*] refer to the six sense faculties of seeing, hearing, smelling, tasting, touching, and the thinking-mind; and the six sense-objects: sights, sounds, scents, flavors, tangible objects, and ideas. The "realms" are eighteen: the six sense faculties, the six sense-objects, and the six consciousnesses. The essential nature embraces all of these dharmas, and so is called the "storehouse-consciousness." If you give rise to a thought, consciousness "turns," and the six consciousnesses are stirred to "go out" the six sense faculties and perceive the six sense-objects. Thus, the eighteen realms are activated from the essential nature.

If the essential nature deviates, it creates the eighteen wrongs. If the essential nature is true and right, it creates the eighteen rights. Misusing it is the activity of living beings; using it well, this is the activity of a Buddha. How does this [differing] usage come about? It all comes from the essential nature.

The external world has five insentient complementary pairings: heaven and earth, sun and moon, light and darkness, yin and yang, water and fire. These are the five complementary pairings.

The characteristics of phenomenal things can be expressed in twelve complementary pairings: words and objects, being and non-being, material and immaterial, perceptible and imperceptible, defiled and undefiled, matter and emptiness, motion and stillness, pure and turbid, mundane and sacred, clergy and laity, old and young, and large and small. These are the twelve complementary pairings.

There are nineteen complementary pairings arising from the essential nature: strengths and weaknesses, deviating and true, foolish and discerning, deluded and wise, scattered and focused, kind and cruel, moral and dissolute, deceptive and genuine, real and vain, biased and fair, afflictions and bodhi, permanent and impermanent, compassion and malice, joy and resentment, generous and stingy, advance and retreat, birth and death, the Dharma-body and the physical body, the Transformed-body and the Reward-body. These are the nineteen complementary pairs.

The Master said:

If you understand and know how to use these thirty-six complementary pairings, you can string together all the teachings in the Sutras, and whether coming or going, you avoid both extremes. Use your essential nature in discoursing with others. Outwardly, be unattached to appearances while right in the middle of appearances. Inwardly, be empty without clinging to emptiness. If you cling to appearances you will just compound your wrong views; if you cling to emptiness, you will only magnify your ignorance.

Those who cling to emptiness repudiate the sutras by insisting you should just talk, and that written works are useless. If they say there is no need for written works, then they shouldn't speak either, because written words are just symbols for the spoken word. They also claim that their direct Way is not based on written works, yet as soon as they set up these two words, "not based," they are writing words. When they see the teachings of others, they slander them, saying they are attached to writings. You should realize that self-delusion is one thing, but slandering the sutras quite another. Do not demean the sutras; if you do, your mistake will result in countless obstructions.

People who attach to external appearances, and moreover practice this way in search of truth, or who extensively set up religious training centers, and preach about errors and evils of existence and nothingness, will not see their fundamental nature even in aeons.

Just listen, understand, and cultivate according to the teachings. Do not try to completely stop all thought, because that will only obstruct the natural [flowing of] the Way. And if people just listen and learn, but do not cultivate, it will have the adverse effect of increasing misunderstanding.

Simply cultivate according to the teaching, and do not cling to appearances when explaining it. All of you, if you understand, then so speak, so engage, so practice, and so act—and you will never stray from the original source.

If someone asks a question about the meaning of "existence," answer with "non-existence." If you are asked about "non-existence," answer with "existence." Asked about the ordinary life, answer with the holy life. Asked about the holy life, answer with the ordinary life. The two are relative to each other, thus disclosing the meaning of the Middle Way. If you answer every question in this complementary fashion, you will not go wrong.

Suppose someone asks, "What is darkness?" You should answer, "Light is the cause, and darkness is the condition; when light disappears, there is darkness. Brightness reveals the dark; and darkness reveals the light."

Since these contrasting pairs mutually complement each other, they affirm the principle of the Middle Way. Answer every question in this way. Later, when you pass on the Dharma, pass it on in this way, and you will never stray from the source of our teaching.

In the seventh month of the year Renzi, the first year of the Taiji and Yanhe reigns [712 c.e.], the Master sent his disciples to The Nation's Gratitude [Guoen] Monastery in Xin Province to construct a stupa. (*This year, 712, was changed during the fifth month, to be called Yanhe. In the eighth month, when the new emperor Xuanzong took the throne, he changed the year period to Xiantian, 'Preceding Heaven,' but then again renamed it the following year as Kaiyuan, 'The Beginning.' Other text[s] have it taking place during the Xiantian, but this is incorrect.*) He ordered them to hurry along the work, and the unveiling took place by the end of the summer the following year.

On the first day of the seventh month he gathered his disciples together and said, "Next month, I want to leave this world. If you have any doubts, you will have to ask me about them soon, so that I can resolve them for you and end your confusion. After I go, there will be no one to teach you."

Hearing this, Fahai and the others wept; Shenhui alone remained emotionally composed and did not cry.

The Master said:

> Little Master Shenhui, only you have gained the equanimity to remain unmoved. Facing good or bad states, blame and praise—sorrow and joy do not stir in you. Not one of the rest of you has attained this—what Way have you been cultivating all these years on this mountain? Who are you crying for so sadly now? Are you worried that I don't know where I am going? I myself know where I am going. If I didn't know where I was going, I wouldn't have been able to inform you ahead of time. No doubt you are crying because you don't know where I am going. But if you knew where I was going, you wouldn't be crying.
>
> The Dharma-nature fundamentally has no birth and death; no coming or going. All of you sit down, and I will recite a verse for you, called "The True-False, Movement-in-Stillness Verse." Recite this verse from memory, and you and I will be of one mind. Cultivate according to it and you will never lose the source of our teaching.

The group of monks bowed and implored the Master to recite his verse. It went:

> *There is nothing real and solid about anything,*
> *Do not view anything as true,*
> *If you regard anything as "real and true,"*
> *This is just a "view": utterly unreal.*

If you can embrace the true yourself,
Just being free of any falseness is the true mind.
Your own mind entangled in the false,
Then nothing's true—where else would you find the true?

Sentient beings can move about,
Insentient things are immobile;
If you cultivate a practice of immobility,
You will be like insentient things: frozen.

If you seek true stillness,
It is movement-in-stillness;
Not moving immobilizes, deadens,
And insentient things lack the Buddha-seed.

Skillfully discerning amid all appearances,
Yet not being turned by them is the cardinal meaning;
The ability to discern in this way
Is itself the true nature at work.

I tell you, Students of the Way:
Exert yourselves; and take heed:
Do not cling to understandings bound up in birth and death,
Right at the gateway to the Supreme vehicle.

If you resonate with these words,
Then let's talk of Buddhahood together.
If there is no resonance,
Then put your palms together and just be happy.

The root-source of this teaching is non-contention;
Arguing is not the meaning of the Way;
For in clinging to or opposing the teaching,
The essential nature embraces birth and death.

Having heard this verse, his disciples all bowed. They understood its meaning. They were determined to cultivate in accord with the teaching and end all arguing and contention.

Realizing that the Great Master would not remain in the world for long, the senior-seated Fahai bowed again and asked, "After the Master leaves this world who will inherit the robe and teaching?"

The Master replied:

> The lectures I have given during the time I was at Great Brahma Monastery [Dafan Si] have been transcribed and circulated. Call them *The Dharma Jewel Platform Sutra*. Preserve it and pass it along. To liberate the myriad living beings, just follow these teachings; they can be called the correct Dharma. I will bequeath the teaching, but I will not bequeath the robe.
>
> This is because your roots of faith are pure, mature. You are confident and free of doubts; you are capable of the great task. So, in keeping with the intention of the First Patriarch, Bodhidharma, the robe is not to be handed on. His verse of bequeathal went:
>
> > *I originally came to this land*
> > *To transmit the Dharma and liberate living beings*
> > *One flower will open into five petals,*
> > *The fruit will all ripen by itself.*

The Master added:

> All of you Good and Wise Advisors, each of you, clear your mind and listen as I explain the Dharma: If you wish to realize perfect wisdom, you must master the "single-mark samadhi," and the "single-practice samadhi." If you do not attach to appearances wherever you are, and do not become attracted to or averse to them, neither grasping nor rejecting, and are untroubled by gain, success,

failure and the like; but instead, in the midst of all things remain calm, composed, fluid and adaptable; modest and not aggressive, quiet in mind with few desires, then you have mastered the "single-mark samadhi."

If no matter where you are, whether you are walking, standing, sitting, or lying down, you can maintain a sincere, straightforward and direct singleness of mind that never leaves the place of awakening, the real Pure Land—this is called the "single-practice samadhi."

Someone who masters these two samadhis is like earth holding seeds which stored in the ground, nurture and grow, mature and ripen into fruit. So it is with the "single-mark" and "single-practice" samadhi. My teaching now is like the seasonal rains everywhere falling and moistening the earth. Your buddha-nature is like the seeds which sprout and grow when moistened by the rain. Those who get the meaning of my teaching will surely realize awakening; those who take up my practice, will definitely realize this sublime "fruit." Listen to my verse:

The mind-ground holds every seed,
Under the falling rain, they all sprout.
Caring for the flowers is the direct awakening,
And the "fruit" of bodhi ripens on its own.

After reciting this verse, the Master said:

This Dharma is non-dual, and the mind is just the same. The Way is pure, pristine, and unmarked. All of you be careful not to "contemplate pure stillness" or a vacant mind. The mind is fundamentally pure; with nothing to grasp or reject. Each of you work hard; and try your best wherever circumstances take you.

Then, all the assembled disciples bowed and withdrew.

On the eighth day of the seventh month, the Master suddenly said to his disciples, "I want to go back to Xin Province. Get a boat ready quickly!" The whole community cried out and begged him to stay, but the Master said, "All Buddhas appear in the world and even appear to pass away. Whatever comes, must go—this is eternally true. This physical body of mine must return somewhere." The assembled group said, "Master, you are leaving, but sooner or later might you come back?" The Master said, "Falling leaves return to the root; who can say when they will return?"

They further asked, "Who was given the 'Treasure of Genuine-Dharma-Discernment'?"[41] The Master replied, "Whoever realizes the Way has it; those with an unattached mind get it." They asked, "Will there be any troubles in the future?"

The Master answered:

Five or six years after my passing, someone will come to take my head. Listen to my prediction:

[Wishing to] make offerings to the parent with bowed head,
Food in the mouth is a must;
When the difficulty of M'an arises,
The officials will be Yang and Liu.

The Master also said:

Seventy years after I leave, two bodhisattvas will come from the East. One will be a monk, the other a layman. They will actively teach as contemporaries, establishing my teaching, restoring the monasteries, and enabling the Dharma to flourish for posterity.

41 *zheng fa yan zang* 正法眼藏. An allusion to the "robe and bowl," but also implies one who has the accomplishment and authority to recognize, validate, and certify (*zheng ming* 證明) the awakening of others. As an example, see chapter 7, Chan Master Xuanjue's encounter.

Someone further asked, "Please tell us, how many generations have passed along the teaching since the first Buddhas and Patriarchs appeared in the world?"

The Master replied:

Since the past, numberless Buddhas have responded to the needs of the world—too many to be counted. For the moment, however, I will begin with the last seven Buddhas. In the past "Adorned Aeon," there were: Vipasyin Buddha, Sikhin Buddha, and Visvabhu Buddha. In the present "Distinguished Aeon" there have been Krakucchanda Buddha, Kanakamuni Buddha, Kasyapa Buddha, and Shakyamuni Buddha—these were the seven Buddhas. From Shakyamuni Buddha, the transmission went through:

Venerable Mahakasyapa
Venerable Ananda
Venerable Sanavasa
Venerable Upagupta
Venerable Dhrtaka
Venerable Micchaka
Venerable Vasumitra
Venerable Buddhanandi
Venerable Punyamitra
Venerable Parsva
Venerable Punyayasas
Venerable Asvaghosa
Venerable Kapimala
Venerable Nagarjuna
Venerable Kanadeva
Venerable Rahulata

Venerable Sanghanandi

Venerable Jayasata

Venerable Kumarata

Venerable Jayata

Venerable Vasubandhu

Venerable Manora

Venerable Haklena

Venerable Sinha

Venerable Vasasita

Venerable Punyamitra

Venerable Prajnatara

Venerable Bodhidharma
   [In China, the first Patriarch]

Great Master Huike

Great Master Sengcan

Great Master Daoxin

Great Master Hongren

And I, Huineng, am the thirty-third Patriarch. Thus, from the beginning each patriarch had his successor. In the future, pass it along accordingly. Do not neglect this.

On the third day of the eighth month of the year Guichou, the second year of the Xiantian reign [713 C.E.] *(At the 12th month, the year was changed to Kai Yuan)*, following a vegetarian meal offering at Nation's Gratitude [Guoen] Monastery, the Master said, "Each of you take your seat; I am going to say farewell." Fahai asked, "What teaching will you leave behind so that people in later generations who are lost and confused will be able to discover their buddha-nature?"

The Master said:

All of you, please listen carefully. In the future, if people who are lost and confused can recognize living beings, they will [find] the buddha-nature. If they don't get to know living beings, they could seek for the Buddha throughout endless aeons and never meet him. I am now teaching you: recognize the living beings of your own mind—the buddha-nature is found right within your own mind. If you wish to see the Buddha, simply come to know these living beings. For it is these living beings who have lost sight of the Buddha, not the Buddha who has lost sight of living beings.

When awakened to the essential nature, the living being is a Buddha. Confused about your essential nature, the "buddha" is a living being.

If your essential nature is balanced and centered, the living being is a Buddha. When your essential nature deviates off course, the "buddha" is a living being.

If your mind is devious and crooked, the "buddha" is concealed within the living being. But with one thought balanced and trued, the living being becomes a Buddha. Our own mind itself holds the Buddha, and this inherent Buddha is the real Buddha. If our own mind did not have its own inherent Buddha, where could the real Buddha be sought? Your own mind is the Buddha. Never doubt this! There is nothing that can be established outside of this mind; for the mind gives rise to the myriad dharmas. Therefore, the Sutra says, "The mind aroused, then all dharmas arise. The mind stilled, all dharmas are stilled."

Now I am going to leave you with a farewell verse, called "The Real Buddha of Your Own Nature." If people of later generations understand its meaning, they will spontaneously see their original mind and realize Buddhahood. The verse goes:

The true "as-it-is" essential nature is the real Buddha,
Wrong views, the three poisons, enthrone a demon.

Lost and confused, the demons own the house,
Seeing true and straight, the Buddha's in the home.

Wrong views, the three poisons, stirred up within the nature,
Just invite the demons to abide,

Right views, true seeing purges the three poisons,
And the demon turns into a Buddha—for real, not false.

Dharma-body, Reward-body, Transformed-bodies:
Fundamentally the three are one.

Seeing this for yourself right within your own nature,
Is the seed of awakening and gaining Buddhahood.

The pure nature arises from the Transformed-body;
This natural purity is ever-present within the Transformed-body;
This nature leads the Transformed-body along the right path
Until it arrives, perfect and complete, truly never-ending.

Lust actually stems from the pure nature;
Just turn back lust—natural purity wholly restored.
Each of you within your own nature, let go the five desires;
Immediately see your nature—this is real and true.

If you encounter this Direct Teaching in your lifetime,
You will immediately understand your essential nature,
And behold the World-Honored One.

If you wish to cultivate, and aspire to become a Buddha,
You won't know where to find this truth
Unless you discover it within your own mind.

Possessing this truth is the seed for becoming a Buddha,
But if you fail to recognize your inherent nature,
And then seek for the Buddha outside,
With this approach you will always be the fool.

I now leave behind the direct teaching.
To become free, people must cultivate themselves;
I announce to you and future seekers of the Way:
If you fail to see this; you will miss it by a long, long way.

After the Master had recited this verse, he said:

All of you; take care. After I pass away, don't indulge in worldly sentiment. If you cry tears like rain, receive condolences, or wear mourning garments, you are no longer my disciples; all of this runs counter to the Teaching. Just recognize your original mind and see your fundamental nature. That nature is neither active nor still, it neither comes nor goes. It is both unborn and undying, it goes beyond right or wrong, and it neither stays nor leaves.

Because I fear in your present state of confusion, you may misunderstand my meaning, I will teach you again, so that you might see your nature.

If after my demise, you cultivate according to this, it will be as if I were still here. But if you go against my teaching it would be of no use even if I were here.

Then he gave another verse:

Firm and steady: not "cultivating" good;
Light and happy: doing no evil;
Calm and clear: no "dusty" sights and sounds;
Vast, vast: the unbound liberated mind.

After reciting this verse the Master meditated until the third watch. Then, all at once he said to his close disciples, "I'm leaving!" And instantly he departed. At that moment a rare fragrance filled the room. A white rainbow linked the earth with the heavens and the trees of the forest turned white. The nearby animals and the birds cried out with grieving sounds.

In the eleventh month a dispute arose among the officers, disciples, sangha and laity of the counties of Guang, Shao, and Xin, over who should receive the Master's "true body." Since they could not resolve their conflicting claims, they lit incense and prayed that the incense smoke would indicate the place where the Master should be laid to rest. The smoke traveled in the direction of Caoxi. And so on the thirteenth day of the eleventh month, the casket and robe and bowl he had inherited were moved back there.

In the following year, on the twenty-fifth day of the seventh month, the Master's body was removed from the casket and disciple Fangbian anointed it with incense paste. Remembering the prediction about the taking of his head, the Master's disciples securely wrapped his neck with sheets of iron and lacquered cloth to protect it and placed his body in the stupa. Suddenly a white light appeared within the stupa, radiated into the sky and only faded away after three days. The provincial governor of Shao reported this to the emperor and was commissioned to set up a stone memorial tablet summarizing the Master's spiritual life.

The Master lived for seventy-six years. He inherited the robe when he was twenty-four and ordained at thirty-nine. He taught the Dharma for thirty-seven years to benefit living beings. He passed on his Dharma to forty-three successors, while those who awakened to the Way and rose above the ordinary were beyond counting. The robe entrusted to him coming down from Bodhidharma, *(finely textured cottony material from India)* and the ceremonial robe and crystal bowl gifted to him by the Emperor Zhongzong, the life-like image sculpted by Fangbian, and other religious implements were permanently housed at Jewel-Wood Monastery.

This *Platform Sutra* has been passed along to reveal the source teachings, to honor the Three Treasures, and for the benefit of all living beings.

~ END ~

A Brief Account of the Life of the Venerable Master Hsüan Hua (1918–1995)

Author of the Preface and Inspiration for this Translation

One of the most eminent Chinese Buddhist masters of the twentieth century, the Venerable Master Hsüan Hua (*Xuanhua*, 1918–1995) was a monastic reformer and the first Chinese master to teach Buddhism to large numbers of Westerners. During his long career he emphasized the primacy of the monastic tradition, the essential role of moral education, the need for Buddhists to ground themselves in traditional spiritual practice and authentic scripture, and the importance of respect and understanding among religions. To attain these goals, he focused on clarifying the essential principles of the Buddha's original teachings, on establishing a properly ordained monastic community, on organizing and supporting the translation of the Buddhist Canon into English and other languages, and on the establishment of schools, religious training programs, and programs of academic research and teaching.

Born in 1918 into a peasant family in a small village south of Harbin, in northeast China, the Venerable Master was the youngest of eight children. His father's surname was Bai, and his mother's maiden name was Hu. His mother was a vegetarian, and throughout her life she held to the practice of reciting the name of the Buddha Amitabha. When the Venerable Master formally became a Buddhist, in his mid-teens, he was given the Dharma name Anci (*"Peace and Compassion"*), and after becoming a monk, he was also known as

To Lun (*Dulun*—"*Liberator from the Wheel of Rebirth*"). Upon granting him the Dharma-seal of the Weiyang (also pronounced *Guiyang*) Chan lineage, the Elder Chan Master Xuyun (1840–1959) bestowed upon him the Dharma-transmission name Hsüan Hua (*Xuanhua*—"*Proclaim and Transform*").

When the Venerable Master was a child, he followed his mother's example, eating only vegetarian food and reciting the Buddha's name. When he was eleven years old, upon seeing a dead baby lying on the ground, he awakened to the fundamental significance of birth and death and the impermanence of all phenomena. He then resolved to become a monk and practice on the Buddhist Path, but he acquiesced to his mother's request that he not do so until after her death. When he was twelve, he obtained his parents' permission to travel extensively in search of a true spiritual teacher.

At the age of fifteen, the Venerable Master went to school for the first time, and when he was sixteen, he started lecturing on the Buddhist Sutras to help his fellow villagers who were illiterate but who wanted to learn about the Buddha's teachings. He was not only diligent and focused but possessed a photographic memory, and so he was able to memorize the Four Books and the Five Classics of the Confucian tradition. He had also studied traditional Chinese medicine, astrology, divination, physiognomy, and the scriptures of the great religions. When he was seventeen, he established a free school, in which, as the lone teacher, he taught some thirty impoverished children and adults.

At the age of eighteen, after only two and a half years of schooling, he left school to care for his terminally ill mother. He was nineteen when she died, and for three years he honored her memory by sitting in meditation beside her grave in a hut made of sorghum stalks. During this time, while reading *The Lotus Sutra,* he experienced a profound awakening. Subsequently, while seated in deep meditation, he had a vision of the Sixth Chan Buddhist Patriarch Huineng (638–713 C.E.). In his vision, Master Huineng came to visit him and to give him the mission of bringing Buddhism to the Western world.

At the end of his period of mourning, the Venerable Master took as his teacher Chan Buddhist Master Changzhi, and he entered Three Conditions Monastery as a novice monk. Chan Master Changzhi subsequently bequeathed to him the Dharma of the Jinding Pilu Chan lineage. During this time, the Master devoted himself not only to meditation but also to the study of the Buddhist scriptural tradition and to the mastery of all the major schools of Chinese Buddhism.

After a period of solitary meditation in the Changbai Mountains, the Master in 1946 began the long journey to the south of China. In 1947, he received full ordination as a monk at the Buddhist holy mountain Putuoshan. In 1948, after over two thousand miles of travel, the Master arrived at Nanhua Monastery and bowed to Chan Master Xuyun (1840–1959), China's most widely revered enlightened master. From him the Master received the 'mind-seal' certification, verifying his awakening, and later a more formal transmission of the Dharma of the Weiyang lineage of the Chan School.

In 1949 the Master left China for Hong Kong. There he taught meditation, lectured on the Buddhist Sutras, and sponsored their printing. He also commissioned the making of images of Buddhas and Bodhisattvas, and aided monastic refugees from mainland China. During these years in Hong Kong, he also built Western Bliss Garden Monastery (*Xi Le Yuan*), established the Buddhist Lecture Hall (*Fojiao Jiangtang*), and rebuilt and renovated Flourishing Compassion Monastery (*Ci Xing Si*).

In 1962, he traveled to the United States at the invitation of his Hong Kong disciples who were then living in the San Francisco Bay Area, and he began lecturing at the San Francisco Buddhist Lecture

Hall (*Sanfanshi Fojiao Jiangtang*), which had been previously set up as a branch of the Hong Kong Buddhist Lecture Hall (*Xianggang Fojiao Jiangtang*). As the community at the Buddhist Lecture Hall in San Francisco grew, both in size and in diversity, the institution's name was changed to the Sino-American Buddhist Association. In 1970, the Venerable Master moved from Chinatown to the newly established Gold Mountain Monastery (*Jinshan Si*) located in the Mission District of San Francisco. In 1975, the Master established the organization's first branch monastery—Gold Wheel Temple (*Jinlun Si*) in Los Angeles; and in 1976 he established the new headquarters as well, the City of Ten Thousand Buddhas (*Wan Fo Cheng*) in Ukiah, California. Then in 1984 the organization's name was changed from the Sino-American Buddhist Association to the Dharma Realm Buddhist Association.

In the summer of 1968, the Master began the intensive training of a group of Americans, most of them university students. In 1969, he astonished the monastic community of Taiwan by sending there, for complete ordination, two American women and three American men whom he had ordained as novices. They were the first Americans of that period to become fully ordained Buddhist monks and nuns. During subsequent years, the Venerable Master trained and oversaw the ordination of hundreds of individuals, both Asians and Westerners who came to California from every part of the world to study with him. These monastic disciples now teach in the twenty-three temples, monasteries and convents that the Venerable Master and his disciples founded in the United States, Canada, Australia, and several Asian countries.

The Venerable Master was determined to transmit to the West the correct teachings of Buddhism, and he categorically rejected what he considered to be corrupt practices that had become widespread in

China. He guided his disciples in distinguishing between genuine, scripture-based practices that were useful and in accord with common sense, as opposed to ritual superstitions that were unwholesome cultural accretions.

Among the many reforms in monastic practice that he instituted was his insistence that his monastic disciples accord with the ancient practice of wearing the monastic robe or precept-sash (*kaṣāya*) as a sign of membership in the monastic Sangha. He himself followed, and required his monastic disciples to follow, the prohibition against eating after noon. He considered a vegetarian diet to be of paramount importance. He encouraged his disciples among the Sangha to join him in following the Buddha's beneficial ascetic practices of eating only one meal a day and of never lying down. Of his monastic disciples he expected strict purity, and he encouraged his lay disciples to adhere to the five precepts of the Buddhist laity.

Although he understood English well and spoke it when necessary, the Master almost always lectured in Chinese. His aim was to encourage his Western disciples to learn Chinese and his Chinese disciples to learn English, so that together they could help to fulfill his wish that the Buddhist Canon be translated into other languages. So far, the Buddhist Text Translation Society he founded has published well over a hundred volumes of translations, including several of the major Mahayana Sutras with the Master's commentaries.

As an educator, the Venerable Master was tireless. At the City of Ten Thousand Buddhas, he established formal training programs for monastics and for laity, elementary and secondary schools for boys and for girls, and Dharma Realm Buddhist University. From 1968 to the early 1990's he himself gave lectures on Sutras at least once a day, and he traveled extensively on speaking tours. Responding to requests from Buddhists around the world, the Venerable Master led delegations to Hong Kong, Taiwan, India, Southeast Asia, and Europe to propagate the Dharma. He also traveled to Burma, Thailand, Malaysia, Australia, and South America. His presence drew a multitude of the faithful everywhere he went. He was also often invited to lecture at universities and academic conferences.

The Venerable Master was a pioneer in building bridges between different Buddhist communities. Wishing to heal the ancient divide between Mahayana Buddhism and Theravada Buddhism, he invited distinguished Theravada monks to the City of Ten Thousand Buddhas to share the duties of full ordination and transmission of the monastic precepts, which the two traditions hold in common.

He also insisted on inter-religious respect and actively promoted interfaith dialogue. He stressed commonalities in religious traditions, above all their emphasis on proper and compassionate conduct. In 1976, together with his friend Paul Cardinal Yubin, who had been archbishop of Nanjing and who was the Chancellor of the Catholic Furen University in Taiwan, he made plans for an Institute for World Religions that came to fruition in Berkeley in 1994.

In 1990, at the invitation of Buddhists in several European countries, the Venerable Master led a large delegation on a European Dharma tour, knowing full well that, because of his ill health at the time, the rigors of the trip would shorten his life. However, as always he considered the Dharma more important than his very life. After his return, his health gradually deteriorated, yet, while quite ill, he made another major tour, this time to Taiwan, in 1993.

In Los Angeles, on June 7, 1995 at the age of 77, the Venerable Master left this world. When he was alive, he craved nothing, seeking neither fame nor wealth nor power. His every thought and every action were for the sake of bringing true happiness to all sentient beings. In his final instructions he said: "After I depart, you can recite

The Avatamsaka Sutra and the name of the Buddha Amitabha for however many days you would like, perhaps seven days or forty-nine days. After cremating my body, scatter all my remains in the air. I do not want you to do anything else at all. Do not build me any pagodas or memorials. I came into the world without anything; when I depart, I still do not want anything, and I do not want to leave any traces in the world. . . . From emptiness I came; to emptiness I am returning."

The Venerable Master Hsüan Hua

The Venerable Master Hsüan Hua's Eighteen Great Vows

1. I vow that I will not realize right enlightenment as long as even one Bodhisattva in the three periods of time throughout the ten directions of the Dharma Realm, to the very ends of empty space, has yet not become a Buddha.

2. I vow that I will not realize right enlightenment as long as even one Solitary Sage in the three periods of time throughout the ten directions of the Dharma Realm, to the very ends of empty space, has yet not become a Buddha.

3. I vow that I will not realize right enlightenment as long as even one Hearer of the Teaching in the three periods of time throughout the ten directions of the Dharma Realm, to the very ends of empty space, has yet not become a Buddha.

4. I vow that I will not realize right enlightenment as long as even one god in the Three Realms has yet not become a Buddha.

5. I vow that I will not realize right enlightenment as long as even one human being in the worlds of the ten directions has yet not become a Buddha.

6. I vow that I will not realize right enlightenment as long as even one asura among people and gods has yet not become a Buddha.

7. I vow that I will not realize right enlightenment as long as even one animal has yet not become a Buddha.

8. I vow that I will not realize right enlightenment as long as even one hungry ghost has yet not become a Buddha.

9. I vow that I will not realize right enlightenment as long as even one being in the hells has yet not become a Buddha.

10. I vow that I will not realize right enlightenment as long as even one being in the Three Realms who has taken refuge with me has yet not become a Buddha—whether that being is a god, ascetic master, human, asura, or animal that swims or flies, or whether a dragon, beast, ghost, or other inhabitant of the spirit-realm.

11. I vow to dedicate all the blessings and happiness that that I am due to enjoy to all the beings of the Dharma Realm.

12. I vow to fully take upon myself all the anguish and hardship that all the beings in the Dharma Realm are due to suffer.

13. I vow to appear in innumerable kinds of bodies in order to reach the minds of all the beings throughout the universe who do not believe in the Buddha's Dharma, so that I may cause them to correct their faults and become good, to repent and to start anew, to take refuge with the Three Jewels and finally to become Buddhas.

14. I vow that any being who sees my face or simply hears my name will immediately resolve to awaken and to follow the Path all the way to Buddhahood.

15. I vow to respectfully observe the Buddha's instructions and to maintain the practice of eating only one meal a day.

16. I vow to bring all beings everywhere to enlightenment by teaching each in accord with the various capabilities of each.

17. I vow, in this very life, to open the five spiritual eyes and to gain the six spiritual powers and the freedom to fly.

18. I vow to make certain that that all my vows are fulfilled.

To these personal vows he added the universal vows of the Bodhisattva:

Though Living beings are countless, I vow to liberate them all.

Though Afflictions are endless, I vow to end them all.

Though Dharma-methods can't be numbered; still, I vow to learn them all.

Though The Buddha's Path is unsurpassed, I vow to realize it.

六祖大師法寶壇經

六祖大師法寶壇經略序

唐釋法海撰

大師名惠能，父盧氏，諱行瑫。母李氏，誕師於唐貞觀十二年，戊戌，二月八日子時。時毫光騰空，異香滿室。

黎明，有二異僧造謁，謂師之父曰：夜來生兒，專為安名，可^上惠^下能也。
父曰：何名惠能？
僧曰：惠者，以法惠施眾生。能者，能作佛事。言畢而出，不知所之。
師不飲乳，夜遇神人灌以甘露。

既長，年二十有四，聞經悟道，往黃梅求印可。五祖器之，付衣法，令嗣祖位。時，龍翔元年辛酉歲也。南歸隱遯一十六年。

至儀鳳元年，丙子，正月八日，會印宗法師，(詰論玄奧)[1]，印宗悟契師旨。

---

[1] 此句取自《大正藏》第四十八冊中的《六祖大師緣起外記》經文，原全唐文並無此句。

是月十五日，普會四眾，為師薙髮。二月八日，集諸名德，授具足戒。西京智光律師為授戒師，蘇州慧靜律師為羯磨，荊州通應律師為教授，中天耆多羅律師為說戒，西國蜜多三藏為證戒。

其戒壇，乃宋朝求那跋陀羅三藏刱建。立碑曰：後當有肉身菩薩於此收戒。又，梁天監元年，智藥三藏自西竺國航海而來，將彼土菩提樹一株，植此壇畔。亦預誌曰：後一百七十年，有肉身菩薩於此樹下開濱上乘，度無量眾，真傳佛心印之法主也。師至是祝髮受戒，及與四眾開示單傳之法旨，一如昔讖。

(以天監元年壬五歲，考至唐儀鳳元年丙子，是得一百七十有五年。)

次年春，師辭眾歸寶林，印宗與緇白，送者千餘人，直至曹溪。時荊州通應律師，與學者數百人，依師而往。至曹溪寶林，覩堂宇湫隘，不足容眾，欲廣之。遂謁里人陳亞仙曰：老僧欲就檀越，求坐具地，得不？

仙曰：和尚坐具幾許濶？祖出坐具示之，亞仙唯然。祖以坐具一展，盡罩曹溪四境，四天王現身，坐鎮四方。今寺境有天王嶺，因茲而名。

仙曰：知和尚法力廣大，但吾高祖墳墓並在此地，他日造墓，幸望存留，餘願盡捨，永為寶坊。然此地乃生龍白象來脈，只可平天，不可平地。寺後營建，一依其言。

師游墳內山水勝處輒憩，近遂成蘭若一十三所。今曰花果院，隸藉寺門。茲寶林道場，亦先是西國智藥三藏，自南海經曹溪口，掬水而飲，香美，異之。謂其徒曰：此水與西天之水無別，溪源上必有勝地，堪為蘭若。隨流至源上，四顧山水回環，峯巒奇秀。歎曰：宛如西天寶林山也。

乃謂曹溪村居民曰：可於此山建一梵剎。一百七十年後，當有無上法寶，於此演化，得道者如林，宜號寶林。

時韶州牧侯敬中，以其言具表聞奏。上可其請，賜寶林為額，遂成梵宮，落成於梁天監三年。

寺殿前有潭一所，龍常出沒其間，觸撓林木。一日，現形甚巨，波浪洶湧，雲霧陰翳，徒眾皆懼。師叱之曰：爾只能現大身，不能現小身。若為神龍，當能變化，以小現大，以大現小也。其龍忽沒，俄頃復現小身，躍出潭面。師展缽試之，曰：爾且不敢入老僧缽盂裏。龍乃游揚至前，師以缽舀之，龍不能動。

師持缽堂上，與龍說法，龍遂蛻骨而去。其骨長可七寸，首尾角足皆具，留傳寺門。師後以土石堙其潭，今殿前左側，有鐵塔處是也。(龍骨至已卯，寺罹兵火因失，未知所之。)

六祖大師法寶壇經

風旛報恩光孝禪寺住持
嗣祖比丘宗寶編

行由第 ·

時，大師至寶林。韶州韋刺史(名璩)與官僚入山請師出，於城中大梵寺講堂，為眾開緣說法。師陞座次，刺史官僚三十餘人，儒宗學士三十餘人，僧尼道俗一千餘人，同時作禮，願聞法要。

大師告眾曰：善知識，菩提自性，本來清淨，但用此心，直了成佛。

善知識，且聽惠能行由，得法事意。惠能嚴父，本貫范陽，左降流于嶺南，作新州百姓。此身不幸，父又早亡。老母孤遺，移來南海，艱辛貧乏，於市賣柴。時，有一客買柴，使令送至客店。客收去，惠能得錢，却出門外，見一客誦經。惠能一聞經語，心即開悟。

遂問：客誦何經？客曰：《金剛經》。

復問：從何所來，持此經典？

客云：我從蘄州黃梅縣東禪寺來。其寺是五祖忍大師在彼主化，門人一千有餘。我到彼中禮拜，聽受此經。大師常勸僧俗，但持《金剛經》，即自見性，直了成佛。

惠能聞說，宿昔有緣，乃蒙一客，取銀十兩與惠能，令充老母衣糧，教便往黃梅參禮五祖。惠能安置母畢，即便辭違。不經三十餘日，便至黃梅，禮拜五祖。

祖問曰：汝何方人？欲求何物？

惠能對曰：弟子是嶺南新州百姓，遠來禮師，惟求作佛，不求餘物。

祖言：汝是嶺南人，又是獦獠，若為堪作佛？

惠能曰：人雖有南北，佛性本無南北。

獦獠身與和尚不同，佛性有何差別？

五祖更欲與語，且見徒眾總在左右，乃令隨眾作務。惠能曰：惠能啟和尚，弟子自心，常生智慧，不離自性，即是福田。未審和尚教作何務？祖云：這獦獠根性大利，汝更勿言，著槽廠去。

惠能退至後院，有一行者，差惠能破柴踏碓。經八月餘，祖一日忽見惠能曰：吾思汝之見可用，恐有惡人害汝，遂不與汝言。汝知之否？惠能曰：弟子亦知師意，不敢行至堂前，令人不覺。

祖一日喚諸門人總來：吾向汝說，世人生死事大，汝等終日只求福田，不求出離生死苦海。自性若迷，福何可救？汝等各去自看智慧，取自本心般若之性，各作一偈來呈吾看。若悟大意，付汝衣法，為第六代祖。火急速去，不得遲滯，思量即不中用。見性之人，言下須見。若如此者，輪刀上陣，亦得見之。

眾得處分，退而遞相謂曰：我等眾人，不須澄心用意作偈，將呈和尚，有何所益？神秀上座，現為教授師，必是他得。我輩謾作偈頌，枉用心力。餘人聞語，總皆息心。咸言，我等已後依止秀師，何煩作偈？

神秀思惟：諸人不呈偈者，為我與他為教授師。我須作偈，將呈和尚，若不呈偈，和尚如何知我心中見解深淺？我呈偈意，求法即善，覓祖即惡，却同凡心，奪其聖位奚別？若不呈偈，終不得法。大難，大難。

五祖堂前，有步廊三間，擬請供奉盧珍，畫楞伽經變相，及五祖血脈圖，流傳供養。神秀作偈成已，數度欲呈，行至堂前，心中恍惚，遍身汗流，擬呈不得。前後經四日，一十三度呈偈不得。秀乃思惟：不如向廊下書著，從他和尚看見，忽若道好，即出禮拜，云是秀

作。若道不堪，枉向山中數年，受人禮
拜，更修何道？是夜三更，不使人知，
自執燈，書偈於南廊壁間，呈心所見。
偈曰：

> 身是菩提樹，　　心如明鏡臺，
> 時時勤拂拭，　　勿使惹塵埃。

秀書偈了，便却歸房，人總不知。秀復
思惟：五祖明日見偈歡喜，即我與法有
緣。若言不堪，自是我迷，宿業障重，
不合得法。聖意難測。房中思想，坐臥
不安，直至五更。

祖已知神秀入門未得，不見自性。天
明，祖喚盧供奉來，向南廊壁間，繪畫
圖相。忽見其偈，報言：供奉却不用
畫，勞爾遠來。經云，凡所有相，皆是
虛妄。但留此偈，與人誦持。依此偈
修，免墮惡道。依此偈修，有大利益。
令門人炷香禮敬，盡誦此偈，即得見
性。門人誦偈，皆歎善哉。

祖，三更喚秀入堂，問曰：偈是汝作否？秀言：實是秀作，不敢妄求祖位，望和尚慈悲，看弟子有少智慧否？

祖曰：汝作此偈，未見本性，只到門外，未入門內。如此見解，覓無上菩提，了不可得。無上菩提，須得言下識自本心，見自本性，不生不滅。於一切時中，念念自見萬法無滯。一真一切真，萬境自如如。如如之心，即是真實。若如是見，即是無上菩提之自性也。汝且去，一兩日思惟，更作一偈將來吾看。汝偈若入得門，付汝衣法。

神秀作禮而出。又經數日，作偈不成，心中恍惚，神思不安，猶如夢中，行坐不樂。

復兩日，有一童子於碓坊過，唱誦其偈。惠能一聞，便知此偈未見本性。雖未蒙教授，早識大意。遂問童子曰：誦者何偈？

童子曰：爾這獦獠不知。大師言，世人生死事大。欲得傳付衣法，令門人作偈來看。若悟大意，即付衣法為第六祖。神秀上座，於南廊壁上，書無相偈。大師令人皆誦，依此偈修，免墮惡道，依此偈修，有大利益。

惠能曰：(一本有我亦要誦此，結來生緣) 上人，我此踏碓，八箇餘月，未曾行到堂前。望上人引至偈前禮拜。

童子引至偈前禮拜，惠能曰：惠能不識字，請上人為讀。時，有江州別駕，姓張名日用，便高聲讀。惠能聞已，遂言：亦有一偈，望別駕為書。別駕言：汝亦作偈？其事希有。

惠能向別駕言：欲學無上菩提，不得輕於初學。下下人有上上智，上上人有沒意智。若輕人，即有無量無邊罪。別駕言：汝但誦偈，吾為汝書。汝若得法，先須度吾。勿忘此言。

惠能偈曰：

> 菩提本無樹，　明鏡亦非臺。
> 本來無一物，　何處惹塵埃？

書此偈已，徒眾總驚，無不嗟訝，各相謂言：奇哉，不得以貌取人，何得多時，使他肉身菩薩。

祖見眾人驚怪，恐人損害，遂將鞋擦了偈，曰：亦未見性。眾以為然。

次日，祖潛至碓坊，見能腰石舂米，語曰：求道之人，為法忘軀，當如是乎。
乃問曰：米熟也未？
惠能曰：米熟久矣，猶欠篩在。

祖以杖擊碓三下而去。惠能即會祖意，三鼓入室。祖以袈裟遮圍，不令人見，為說《金剛經》。至「應無所住而生其心」，惠能言下大悟，一切萬法，不離自性。

遂啟祖言：何期自性，本自清淨。何期
自性，本不生滅。何期自性，本自具
足。何期自性，本無動搖。何期自性，
能生萬法。

祖知悟本性，謂惠能曰：不識本心，學
法無益。若識自本心，見自本性，即名
丈夫，天人師，佛。

三更受法，人盡不知。便傳頓教及衣
鉢，云：汝為第六代祖，善自護念，廣
度有情，流布將來，無令斷絕。聽吾偈
曰：

　　有情來下種，　　因地果還生，
　　無情既無種，　　無性亦無生。

祖復曰：昔達磨大師，初來此土，人未
之信，故傳此衣，以為信體，代代相
承。法則以心傳心，皆令自悟自解。自
古，佛佛惟傳本體，師師密付本心。衣
為爭端，止汝勿傳。若傳此衣，命如懸

絲。汝須速去，恐人害汝。

惠能啟曰：向甚處去？
祖云：逢懷則止，遇會則藏。

惠能三更領得衣鉢，云：能本是南中人，素不知此山路，如何出得江口？
五祖言：汝不須憂，吾自送汝。

祖相送，直至九江驛。祖令上船，五祖把艣自搖。惠能言：請和尚坐。弟子合搖艣。祖云：合是吾渡汝。

惠能云：迷時師度，悟了自度。度名雖一，用處不同。惠能生在邊方，語音不正，蒙師傳法，今已得悟，只合自性自度。

祖云：如是，如是，以後佛法，由汝大行。汝去三年，吾方逝世。汝今好去，努力向南。不宜速說，佛法難起。

惠能辭違祖已，發足南行。兩月中間，

至大庾嶺 (五祖歸，數日不上堂。眾疑，詣問
曰：和尚少病少惱否？曰：病即無。衣法已南矣。
問：誰人傳授？曰：能者得之。眾乃知焉)。逐後
數百人來，欲奪衣鉢。

一僧俗姓陳，名惠明，先是四品將軍，
性行麄慥，極意參尋。為眾人先，趁及
惠能。惠能擲下衣鉢於石上，云：此衣
表信，可力爭耶？能隱草莽中。惠明
至，提掇不動，乃喚云：行者，行者，
我為法來，不為衣來。

惠能遂出，坐盤石上。惠明作禮云：望
行者為我說法。惠能云：汝既為法而
來，可屏息諸緣，勿生一念，吾為汝說
明。良久。

惠能云：不思善，不思惡，正與麼時，
那箇是明上座本來面目？

惠明言下大悟。復問云：上來密語密意
外，還更有密意否？

惠能云：與汝說者，即非密也。汝若返照，密在汝邊。

明曰：惠明雖在黃梅，實未省自己面目。今蒙指示，如人飲水，冷暖自知。今行者即惠明師也。

惠能曰：汝若如是，吾與汝同師黃梅，善自護持。

明又問：惠明今後向甚處去？

惠能曰：逢袁則止，遇蒙則居。

明禮辭 (明回至嶺下，謂趁眾曰：向陟崔嵬，竟無蹤跡，當別道尋之。趁眾咸以為然。惠明後改道明，避師上字)。

惠能後至曹溪，又被惡人尋逐。乃於四會，避難獵人隊中，凡經一十五載，時與獵人隨宜說法。獵人常令守網，每見生命，盡放之。每至飯時，以菜寄煮肉鍋。或問，則對曰：但喫肉邊菜。

一日思惟：時當弘法，不可終遯。遂出

至廣州法性寺，值印宗法師講《涅槃
經》。時，有風吹旛動，一僧曰：風
動。一僧曰：旛動。議論不已。惠能進
曰：不是風動，不是旛動，仁者心動。
一眾駭然。

印宗延至上席，徵詰奧義。見惠能言簡
理當，不由文字，宗云：行者定非常
人。久聞黃梅衣法南來，莫是行者否？
惠能曰：不敢。宗於是作禮，告請傳來
衣鉢出示大眾。

宗復問曰：黃梅付囑，如何指授？
惠能曰：指授即無。惟論見性，不論禪
定解脫。
宗曰：何不論禪定解脫？
能曰：為是二法，不是佛法。佛法是不
二之法。
宗又問：如何是佛法不二之法？
惠能曰：法師講《涅槃經》，明佛性，
是佛法不二之法。如高貴德王菩薩白佛

言，犯四重禁，作五逆罪，及一闡提等，當斷善根佛性否？佛言善根有二，「一者常，二者無常，佛性非常非無常，是故不斷。」名為不二。一者善，二者不善，佛性非善非不善，是名不二。蘊之與界，凡夫見二，智者了達其性無二，無二之性即是佛性。

印宗聞說，歡喜合掌言：某甲講經，猶如瓦礫。仁者論義，猶如真金。
於是為惠能剃髮，願事為師。
惠能遂於菩提樹下，開東山法門。

惠能於東山得法，辛苦受盡，命似懸絲。今日得與使君官僚，僧尼道俗，同此一會，莫非累劫之緣。亦是過去生中供養諸佛，同種善根，方始得聞如上頓教得法之因。教是先聖所傳，不是惠能自智。願聞先聖教者，各令淨心，聞了各自除疑，如先代聖人無別。

一眾聞法，歡喜作禮而退。

般若第二

次日，韋使君請益。師陞座，告大眾曰：總淨心，念摩訶般若波羅蜜多。

復云：善知識，菩提般若之智，世人本自有之。只緣心迷，不能自悟，須假大善知識，示導見性。當知愚人智人，佛性本無差別，只緣迷悟不同，所以有愚有智。吾今為說摩訶般若波羅蜜法，使汝等各得智慧。志心諦聽，吾為汝說。

善知識，世人終日口念般若，不識自性般若，猶如說食不飽。口但說空，萬劫不得見性，終無有益。

善知識，摩訶般若波羅蜜是梵語，此言大智慧到彼岸。此須心行，不在口念。口念心不行，如幻如化，如露如電。口念心行，則心口相應，本性是佛，離性無別佛。何名摩訶？摩訶是大。心量廣大，猶如虛空，無有邊畔，亦無方圓大

小，亦非青黃赤白，亦無上下長短，亦
無瞋無喜，無是無非，無善無惡，無有
頭尾。諸佛刹土，盡同虛空。世人妙性
本空，無有一法可得。自性真空，亦復
如是。善知識，莫聞吾說空，便即著
空。第一莫著空，若空心靜坐，即著無
記空。

善知識，世界虛空，能含萬物色像，日
月星宿，山河大地，泉源谿澗，草木叢
林，惡人善人，惡法善法，天堂地獄，
一切大海，須彌諸山，總在空中。世人
性空，亦復如是。

善知識，自性能含萬法是大，萬法在諸
人性中。若見一切人，惡之與善，盡皆
不取不捨，亦不染著，心如虛空，名之
為大，故曰摩訶。

善知識，迷人口說，智者心行。又有迷
人，空心靜坐，百無所思，自稱為大。
此一輩人，不可與語，為邪見故。

善知識，心量廣大，遍周法界，用即了了分明，應用便知一切。一切即一，一即一切。去來自由，心體無滯，即是般若。善知識，一切般若智，皆從自性而生，不從外入。莫錯用意，名為真性自用，一真一切真。心量大事，不行小道。口莫終日說空，心中不修此行，恰似凡人自稱國王，終不可得，非吾弟子。

善知識，何名般若？般若者，唐言智慧也。一切處所，一切時中，念念不愚，常行智慧，即是般若行。一念愚即般若絕，一念智即般若生。世人愚迷，不見般若，口說般若，心中常愚，常自言我修般若，念念說空，不識真空。般若無形相，智慧心即是。若作如是解，即名般若智。

何名波羅蜜？此是西國語，唐言到彼岸，解義離生滅。著境生滅起，如水有波浪，即名為此岸。離境無生滅，如水常通流，即名為彼岸，故號波羅蜜。

善知識，迷人口念，當念之時，有妄有非。念念若行，是名真性。悟此法者，是般若法。修此行者，是般若行。不修即凡。一念修行，自身等佛。善知識，凡夫即佛，煩惱即菩提。前念迷即凡夫，後念悟即佛。前念著境即煩惱，後念離境即菩提。

善知識，摩訶般若波羅蜜，最尊最上最第一，無住無往亦無來，三世諸佛從中出。當用大智慧，打破五蘊煩惱塵勞。如此修行，定成佛道，變三毒為戒定慧。

善知識，我此法門，從一般若生八萬四千智慧。何以故？為世人有八萬四千塵勞。若無塵勞，智慧常現，不離自性。悟此法者，即是無念，無憶無著，不起誑妄。用自真如性，以智慧觀照，於一切法不取不捨，即是見性成佛道。

善知識，若欲入甚深法界，及般若三昧者，須修般若行，持誦《金剛般若經》即得見性。當知此經功德，無量無邊，經中分明讚歎，莫能具說。此法門是最上乘，為大智人說，為上根人說。小根小智人聞，心生不信。何以故？譬如大龍下雨於閻浮提，城邑聚落，悉皆漂流如漂棗葉。若雨大海，不增不減。若大乘人，若最上乘人，聞說《金剛經》，心開悟解。故知本性自有般若之智，自用智慧，常觀照故，不假文字。譬如雨水，不從天有，元是龍能興致，令一切眾生，一切草木，有情無情，悉皆蒙潤。百川眾流，却入大海，合為一體。眾生本性般若之智，亦復如是。

善知識，小根之人，聞此頓教，猶如草木根性小者，若被大雨，悉皆自倒，不能增長。小根之人，亦復如是。元有般若之智，與大智人更無差別，因何聞法不自開悟？緣邪見障重，煩惱根深。猶如大雲覆蓋於日，不得風吹，日光不現。般若之智亦無大小，為一切眾生自心迷悟不同，迷心外見，修行覓佛。未悟自性，即是小根。若開悟頓教，不能外修，但於自心常起正見，煩惱塵勞常不能染，即是見性。善知識，內外不住，去來自由，能除執心，通達無礙。能修此行，與般若經本無差別。

善知識，一切修多羅及諸文字，大小二乘，十二部經，皆因人置。因智慧性，方能建立。若無世人，一切萬法本自不有，故知萬法本自人興。一切經書，因人說有。緣其人中有愚有智，愚為小人，智為大人。愚者問於智人，智者與愚人說法。愚人忽然悟解心開，即與智人無別。

善知識，不悟即佛是眾生，一念悟時眾

生是佛，故知萬法盡在自心。何不從自
心中，頓見真如本性？《菩薩戒經》
云：我本元自性清淨，若識自心見性，
皆成佛道。《淨名經》云：即時豁然，
還得本心。

善知識，我於忍和尚處，一聞言下便
悟，頓見真如本性。是以將此教法流
行，令學道者頓悟菩提，各自觀心，自
見本性。若自不悟，須覓大善知識，解
最上乘法者，直示正路。是善知識有大
因緣，所謂化導令得見性。一切善法，
因善知識能發起故。三世諸佛，十二部
經，在人性中本自具有。不能自悟，須
求善知識指示方見。若自悟者，不假外
求。若一向執謂須他善知識方得解脫
者，無有是處。何以故？自心內有知識
自悟。若起邪迷，妄念顛倒，外善知識
雖有教授，救不可得。若起正真般若觀
照，一刹那間，妄念俱滅。若識自性，
一悟即至佛地。

善知識，智慧觀照，內外明徹，識自本心。若識本心，即本解脫。若得解脫，即是般若三昧，即是無念。何名無念？若見一切法，心不染著，是為無念。用即遍一切處，亦不著一切處。但淨本心，使六識出六門，於六塵中無染無雜，來去自由，通用無滯，即是般若三昧，自在解脫，名無念行。若百物不思，當令念絕，即是法縛，即名邊見。

善知識，悟無念法者，萬法盡通。悟無念法者，見諸佛境界。悟無念法者，至佛地位。

善知識，後代得吾法者，將此頓教法門，於同見同行，發願受持。如事佛故，終身而不退者，定入聖位。然須傳授，從上以來默傳分付，不得匿其正法。若不同見同行，在別法中，不得傳付。損彼前人，究竟無益。恐愚人不解，謗此法門，百劫千生，斷佛種性。

善知識，吾有一無相頌，各須誦取，在
家出家，但依此修。若不自修，惟記吾
言，亦無有益。聽吾頌曰：

說通及心通，　　如日處虛空，
唯傳見性法，　　出世破邪宗。
法即無頓漸，　　迷悟有遲疾，
只此見性門，　　愚人不可悉。
說即雖萬般，　　合理還歸一，
煩惱闇宅中，　　常須生慧日。
邪來煩惱至，　　正來煩惱除，
邪正俱不用，　　清淨至無餘。
菩提本自性，　　起心即是妄，
淨心在妄中，　　但正無三障。
世人若修道，　　一切盡不妨，
常自見己過，　　與道即相當。
色類自有道，　　各不相妨惱，
離道別覓道，　　終身不見道。
波波度一生，　　到頭還自懊，
欲得見真道，　　行正即是道。
自若無道心，　　闇行不見道，

若真修道人，　　不見世間過。
若見他人非，　　自非却是左，
他非我不非，　　我非自有過。
但自却非心，　　打除煩惱破，
憎愛不關心，　　長伸兩脚臥。
欲擬化他人，　　自須有方便，
勿令彼有疑，　　即是自性現。
佛法在世間，　　不離世間覺，
離世覓菩提，　　恰如求兔角。
正見名出世　　邪見是世間，
邪正盡打却，　　菩提性宛然。
此頌是頓教，　　亦名大法船，
迷聞經累劫，　　悟則刹那間。

師復曰：今於大梵寺說此頓教，普願法界眾生，言下見性成佛。

時，韋使君與官僚道俗，聞師所說，無不省悟。一時作禮，皆歎善哉，何期嶺南有佛出世。

疑問第三

一日，韋刺史為師設大會齋。齋訖，刺史請師陞座，同官僚士庶肅容再拜，問曰：弟子聞和尚說法，實不可思議。今有少疑，願大慈悲，特為解說。

師曰：有疑即問，吾當為說。

韋公曰：和尚所說，可不是達磨大師宗旨乎？

師曰：是。

公曰：弟子聞，達磨初化梁武帝，帝問云，朕一生造寺度僧，布施設齋，有何功德？達磨言，實無功德。弟子未達此理，願和尚為說。

師曰：實無功德，勿疑先聖之言。武帝心邪，不知正法。造寺度僧，布施設齋，名為求福，不可將福便為功德。功德在法身中，不在修福。

師又曰：見性是功，平等是德。念念無

滯，常見本性，真實妙用，名為功德。內心謙下是功，外行於禮是德。自性建立萬法是功，心體離念是德。不離自性是功，應用無染是德。若覓功德法身，但依此作，是真功德。若修功德之人，心即不輕，常行普敬。心常輕人，吾我不斷，即自無功。自性虛妄不實，即自無德。為吾我自大，常輕一切故。

善知識，念念無間是功，心行平直是德。自修性是功，自修身是德。

善知識，功德須自性內見，不是布施供養之所求也。是以福德與功德別。武帝不識真理，非我祖師有過。

刺史又問曰：弟子常見僧俗念阿彌陀佛，願生西方。請和尚說，得生彼否？願為破疑。

師言：使君善聽，惠能與說。世尊在舍衛城中，說西方引化。經文分明，去此不遠。若論相說，里數有十萬八千，即身中十惡八邪，便是說遠。說遠為其下根，說近為其上智。人有兩種，法無兩般。迷悟有殊，見有遲疾。迷人念佛求生於彼，悟人自淨其心。所以佛言，隨其心淨即佛土淨。使君東方人，但心淨即無罪。雖西方人，心不淨亦有愆。東方人造罪，念佛求生西方。西方人造罪，念佛求生何國？凡愚不了自性，不識身中淨土，願東願西。悟人在處一般，所以佛言，隨所住處恒安樂。

使君心地但無不善，西方去此不遙。若懷不善之心，念佛往生難到。今勸善知識，先除十惡即行十萬，後除八邪乃過八千。念念見性，常行平直，到如彈指，便覩彌陀。

使君但行十善，何須更願往生？不斷十惡之心，何佛即來迎請？若悟無生頓法，見西方只在剎那。不悟，念佛求生，路遙如何得達。惠能與諸人，移西方於剎那間，目前便見。各願見否？

眾皆頂禮云：若此處見，何須更願往生？願和尚慈悲，便現西方，普令得見。

師言：大眾，世人自色身是城，眼耳鼻舌是門，外有五門，內有意門。心是地，性是王。王居心地上，性在王在，性去王無。性在身心存，性去身壞。

佛向性中作，莫向身外求。自性迷即是眾生，自性覺即是佛。慈悲即是觀音，喜捨名為勢至，能淨即釋迦，平直即彌陀。人我是須彌，貪欲是海水，煩惱是波浪，毒害是惡龍，虛妄是鬼神，塵勞是魚鱉。貪瞋是地獄，愚癡是畜生。

善知識，常行十善，天堂便至。除人我，須彌倒。去貪欲，海水竭。煩惱無，波浪滅。毒害除，魚龍絕。自心地

上，覺性如來，放大光明。外照六門清
淨，能破六欲諸天。自性內照，三毒即
除，地獄等罪一時銷滅。內外明徹，不
異西方。不作此修，如何到彼？

大眾聞說，了然見性，悉皆禮拜，俱歎
善哉。唱言：普願法界眾生，聞者一時
悟解。

師言：善知識，若欲修行，在家亦得，
不由在寺。在家能行，如東方人心善。
在寺不修，如西方人心惡。但心清淨，
即是自性西方。

韋公又問：在家如何修行？願為教授。

師言：吾與大眾說無相頌。但依此修，
常與吾同處無別。若不依此修，剃髮出
家於道何益？頌曰：

　　心平何勞持戒，行直何用修禪。

　　恩則孝養父母，義則上下相憐。

讓則尊卑和睦，忍則眾惡無諠。

若能鑽木出火，淤泥定生紅蓮。

苦口的是良藥，逆耳必是忠言。

改過必生智慧，護短心內非賢。

日用常行饒益，成道非由施錢。

菩提只向心覓，何勞向外求玄。

聽說依此修行，西方只在目前。

師復曰：善知識，總須依偈修行，見取自性，直成佛道。時不相待，眾人且散，吾歸曹溪。眾若有疑，却來相問。

時，刺史官僚，在會善男信女，各得開悟，信受奉行。

定慧第四

師示眾云：善知識，我此法門，以定慧為本。大眾勿迷，言定慧別。定慧一體，不是二。定是慧體，慧是定用。即慧之時定在慧，即定之時慧在定。若識此義，即是定慧等學。

諸學道人，莫言先定發慧，先慧發定各別。作此見者，法有二相。口說善語，心中不善。空有定慧，定慧不等。若心口俱善，內外一如，定慧即等。自悟修行，不在於諍。若諍先後，即同迷人，不斷勝負，却增我法，不離四相。

善知識，定慧猶如何等？猶如燈光。有燈即光，無燈即闇。燈是光之體，光是燈之用。名雖有二，體本同一。此定慧法，亦復如是。

師示眾云：善知識，一行三昧者，於一切處，行住坐臥，常行一直心是也。

《淨名》云, 直心是道場。直心是淨土。

莫心行諂曲, 口但說直, 口說一行三昧, 不行直心。但行直心, 於一切法勿有執著。迷人著法相, 執一行三昧, 直言常坐不動, 妄不起心, 即是一行三昧。作此解者, 即同無情, 卻是障道因緣。

善知識, 道須通流, 何以卻滯? 心不住法, 道即通流。心若住法, 名為自縛。若言常坐不動是, 只如舍利弗宴坐林中, 卻被維摩詰訶。

善知識, 又有人教坐, 看心觀靜, 不動不起, 從此置功。迷人不會, 便執成顛。如此者眾, 如是相教, 故知大錯。

師示眾云: 善知識, 本來正教, 無有頓漸, 人性自有利鈍。迷人漸修, 悟人頓契。自識本心, 自見本性, 即無差別。所以立頓漸之假名。

善知識，我此法門，從上以來，先立無念為宗，無相為體，無住為本。

無相者，於相而離相。無念者，於念而無念。無住者，人之本性。於世間善惡好醜，乃至冤之與親，言語觸刺，欺爭之時，並將為空，不思酬害。念念之中，不思前境。若前念今念後念，念念相續不斷，名為繫縛。於諸法上，念念不住，即無縛也。此是以無住為本。

善知識，外離一切相，名為無相。能離於相，即法體清淨。此是以無相為體。

善知識，於諸境上，心不染，曰無念。於自念上，常離諸境，不於境上生心。若只百物不思，念盡除却，一念絕即死，別處受生，是為大錯。學道者思之。若不識法意，自錯猶可，更誤他人。自迷不見，又謗佛經。所以立無念為宗。

善知識，云何立無念為宗？只緣口說見性，迷人於境上有念，念上便起邪見，一切塵勞妄想從此而生。自性本無一法可得，若有所得，妄說禍福，即是塵勞邪見，故此法門立無念為宗。

善知識，無者無何事？念者念何物？無者無二相，無諸塵勞之心。念者念真如本性。真如即是念之體，念即是真如之用。真如自性起念，非眼耳鼻舌能念。真如有性，所以起念。真如若無，眼耳色聲當時即壞。

善知識，真如自性起念，六根雖有見聞覺知，不染萬境，而真性常自在。

故經云，「能善分別諸法相，於第一義而不動。」

坐禪第五

師示眾云：此門坐禪，元不著心，亦不著淨，亦不是不動。

若言著心，心元是妄，知心如幻，故無所著也。若言著淨，人性本淨，由妄念故，蓋覆真如。但無妄想，性自清淨。起心著淨，却生淨妄。妄無處所，著者是妄。淨無形相，却立淨相，言是工夫。作此見者，障自本性，却被淨縛。

善知識，若修不動者，但見一切人時，不見人之是非善惡過患，即是自性不動。

善知識，迷人身雖不動，開口便說他人是非長短好惡，與道違背。若著心著淨，即障道也。

師示眾云：善知識，何名坐禪？此法門中，無障無礙。外於一切善惡境界，心念不起，名為坐。內見自性不動，名為禪。

善知識，何名禪定？外離相為禪，內不亂為定。外若著相，內心即亂。外若離相，心即不亂。本性自淨自定，只為見境，思境即亂。若見諸境，心不亂者，是真定也。

善知識，外離相即禪，內不亂即定。外禪內定，是為禪定。

《菩薩戒經》云，我本元自性清淨。

善知識，於念念中，自見本性清淨，自修自行，自成佛道。

懺悔第六

時，大師見廣韶洎四方士庶，駢集山中聽法，於是陞座，告眾曰：來諸善知識，此事須從自事中起，於一切時，念念自淨其心。自修自行，見自己法身，見自心佛，自度自戒，始得不假到此。既從遠來，一會于此，皆共有緣。今可各各胡跪，先為傳自性五分法身香，次授無相懺悔。

眾胡跪。

師曰：一，戒香。即自心中無非無惡，無嫉妒，無貪瞋，無劫害，名戒香。二，定香。即覩諸善惡境相，自心不亂，名定香。三，慧香。自心無礙，常以智慧觀照自性，不造諸惡。雖修眾善，心不執著，敬上念下，矜恤孤貧，名慧香。四，解脫香。即自心無所攀緣，不思善，不思惡，自在無礙，名解脫香。
五，解脫知見香。自心既無所攀緣善
惡，不可沈空守寂，即須廣學多聞，識
自本心，達諸佛理，和光接物，無我無
人，直至菩提，真性不易，名解脫知見
香。善知識，此香各自內熏，莫向外
覓。

今與汝等授無相懺悔，滅三世罪，令得
三業清淨。善知識，各隨我語，一時
道：弟子等，從前念今念及後念，念念
不被愚迷染。從前所有惡業愚迷等罪，
悉皆懺悔，願一時銷滅，永不復起。

弟子等，從前念今念及後念，念念不被
憍誑染。從前所有惡業憍誑等罪，悉皆
懺悔，願一時銷滅，永不復起。

弟子等，從前念今念及後念，念念不被
嫉妒染。從前所有惡業嫉妒等罪，悉皆
懺悔，願一時銷滅，永不復起。

善知識，已上是為無相懺悔。云何名
懺？云何名悔？

懺者，懺其前愆，從前所有惡業，愚迷
憍誑，嫉妒等罪，悉皆盡懺，永不復
起，是名為懺。

悔者，悔其後過，從今以後，所有惡
業，愚迷憍誑，嫉妒等罪，今已覺悟，
悉皆永斷，更不復作，是名為悔。故稱
懺悔。

凡夫愚迷，只知懺其前愆，不知悔其後
過。以不悔故，前愆不滅，後過又生。
前愆既不滅，後過復又生，何名懺悔？

善知識，既懺悔已，與善知識發四弘誓
願，各須用心正聽。

自心眾生無邊誓願度，自心煩惱無邊誓
願斷，自性法門無盡誓願學，自性無上
佛道誓願成。

善知識，大家豈不道，眾生無邊誓願
度。恁麼道，且不是惠能度。

善知識，心中眾生，所謂邪迷心，誑妄心，不善心，嫉妒心，惡毒心，如是等心，盡是眾生。各須自性自度，是名真度。何名自性自度？即自心中，邪見煩惱愚癡眾生，將正見度。既有正見，使般若智，打破愚癡迷妄眾生，各各自度。邪來正度，迷來悟度，愚來智度，惡來善度。如是度者，名為真度。

又煩惱無邊誓願斷，將自性般若智，除却虛妄思想心是也。

又法門無盡誓願學，須自見性，常行正法，是名真學。

又無上佛道誓願成，既常能下心，行於真正，離迷離覺，常生般若。除真除妄，即見佛性，即言下佛道成。常念修行，是願力法。

善知識，今發四弘願了，更與善知識，授無相三歸依戒。

善知識，歸依覺，兩足尊。歸依正，離欲尊。歸依淨，眾中尊。從今日去，稱覺為師，更不歸依邪魔外道。以自性三寶常自證明。勸善知識歸依自性三寶。

佛者，覺也。法者，正也。僧者，淨也。

自心歸依覺，邪迷不生，少欲知足，能離財色，名兩足尊。

自心歸依正，念念無邪見，以無邪見故，即無人我貢高，貪愛執著，名離欲尊。

自心歸依淨，一切塵勞，愛欲境界，自性皆不染著，名眾中尊。

若修此行，是自歸依。凡夫不會，從日至夜受三歸戒。若言歸依佛，佛在何處？若不見佛，憑何所歸，言却成妄。

善知識，各自觀察，莫錯用心。經文分明言，自歸依佛，不言歸依他佛。自佛

不歸，無所依處。今既自悟，各須歸依
自心三寶，內調心性，外敬他人，是自
歸依也。

善知識，既歸依自三寶竟，各各志心，
吾與說一體三身自性佛，令汝等見三身
了然，自悟自性。總隨我道：於自色
身，歸依清淨法身佛。於自色身，歸依
圓滿報身佛。於自色身，歸依千百億化
身佛。

善知識，色身是舍宅，不可言歸。向者
三身佛，在自性中，世人總有。為自心
迷，不見內性。外覓三身如來，不見自
身中有三身佛。汝等聽說，令汝等於自
身中，見自性有三身佛。此三身佛，從
自性生，不從外得。

何名清淨法身佛？世人性本清淨，萬法
從自性生。思量一切惡事，即生惡行。
思量一切善事，即生善行。如是諸法在
自性中，如天常清，日月常明，為浮雲

蓋覆，上明下暗。忽遇風吹雲散，上下俱明，萬象皆現。世人性常浮游，如彼天雲。

善知識，智如日，慧如月，智慧常明。於外著境，被妄念浮雲蓋覆自性，不得明朗。若遇善知識，聞真正法，自除迷妄，內外明徹，於自性中萬法皆現。見性之人，亦復如是。此名清淨法身佛。

善知識，自心歸依自性，是歸依真佛。自歸依者，除却自性中不善心，嫉妒心，諂曲心，吾我心，誑妄心，輕人心，慢他心，邪見心，貢高心，及一切時中不善之行。常自見己過，不說他人好惡，是自歸依。常須下心，普行恭敬，即是見性通達，更無滯礙，是自歸依。

何名圓滿報身？譬如一燈能除千年闇，一智能滅萬年愚。莫思向前已過，不可得常思於後。念念圓明，自見本性。善惡雖殊，本性無二，無二之性，名為實性。於實性中，不染善惡，此名圓滿報身佛。自性起一念惡，滅萬劫善因。自性起一念善，得恒沙惡盡。直至無上菩提，念念自見，不失本念，名為報身。

何名千百億化身？若不思萬法，性本如空，一念思量，名為變化。思量惡事，化為地獄。思量善事，化為天堂。毒害化為龍蛇。慈悲化為菩薩。智慧化為上界。愚癡化為下方。自性變化甚多，迷人不能省覺，念念起惡，常行惡道。迴一念善，智慧即生，此名自性化身佛。

善知識，法身本具，念念自性自見，即是報身佛。從報身思量，即是化身佛。自悟自修自性功德，是真歸依。皮肉是色身，色身是舍宅，不言歸依也。但悟自性三身，即識自性佛。吾有一無相頌，若能師持，言下令汝積劫迷罪，一時銷滅。頌曰：

迷人修福不修道，只言修福便是道，
布施供養福無邊，心中三惡元來造。

擬將修福欲滅罪，後世得福罪還在，
但向心中除罪緣，各自性中真懺悔。

忽悟大乘真懺悔，除邪行正即無罪，
學道常於自性觀，即與諸佛同一類。

吾祖惟傳此頓法，普願見性同一體，
若欲當來覓法身，離諸法相心中洗。

努力自見莫悠悠，後念忽絕一世休，
若悟大乘得見性，虔恭合掌至心求。

師言：善知識，總須誦取，依此修行，
言下見性，雖去吾千里，如常在吾邊。
於此言下不悟，即對面千里，何勤遠
來。珍重好去。

一眾聞法，靡不開悟，歡喜奉行。

機緣第七

師自黃梅得法，回至韶州曹侯村，人無知者 (他本云，師去時，至曹侯村，住九月餘。然師自言：不經三十餘日便至黃梅。此求道之切，豈有逗留？作去時者非是)。

有儒士劉志略，禮遇甚厚。志略有姑為尼，名無盡藏，常誦《大涅槃經》。師暫聽，即知妙義，遂為解說。尼乃執卷問字，師曰：字即不識，義即請問。尼曰：字尚不識，焉能會義？師曰：諸佛妙理，非關文字。尼驚異之，遍告里中耆德云：此是有道之士，宜請供養。有魏(魏一作晉)武侯玄孫曹叔良及居民，競來瞻禮。

時，寶林古寺，自隋末兵火已廢，遂於故基重建梵宇，延師居之，俄成寶坊。師住九月餘日，又為惡黨尋逐，師乃遯于前山。被其縱火焚草木，師隱身挨入石中得免。石今有師趺坐膝痕，及衣布

之紋，因名避難石。師憶五祖懷會止藏
之囑，遂行隱于二邑焉。

僧法海，韶州曲江人也。初參祖師，
問曰：即心即佛，願垂指諭。
師曰：前念不生即心，後念不滅即佛。
成一切相即心，離一切相即佛。吾若具
說，窮劫不盡。聽吾偈曰：

即心名慧，　即佛乃定，
定慧等持，　意中清淨。
悟此法門，　由汝習性，
用本無生，　雙修是正。

法海言下大悟，以偈讚曰：

即心元是佛，　不悟而自屈，
我知定慧因，　雙修離諸物。

僧法達，洪州人，七歲出家，常誦《法
華經》。來禮祖師，頭不至地。
師訶曰：禮不投地，何如不禮？汝心中
必有一物。蘊習何事耶？

曰：念《法華經》，已及三千部。

師曰：汝若念至萬部，得其經意，不以為勝，則與吾偕行。汝今負此事業，都不知過。聽吾偈曰：

禮本折慢幢，　頭奚不至地？
有我罪即生，　亡功福無比。

師又曰：汝名什麼？

曰：法達。

師曰：汝名法達，何曾達法？

復說偈曰：

汝今名法達，　勤誦未休歇，
空誦但循聲，　明心號菩薩。
汝今有緣故，　吾今為汝說，
但信佛無言，　蓮華從口發。

達聞偈，悔謝曰：而今而後，當謙恭一切。弟子誦《法華經》，未解經義，心常有疑。和尚智慧廣大，願略說經中義理。

師曰：法達，法即甚達，汝心不達。經本無疑，汝心自疑。汝念此經，以何為宗？

達曰：學人根性闇鈍，從來但依文誦念，豈知宗趣？

師曰：吾不識文字，汝試取經誦一遍，吾當為汝解說。

法達即高聲念經，至譬喻品，師曰：止，此經元來以因緣出世為宗，縱說多種譬喻，亦無越於此。何者因緣？經云，「諸佛世尊，唯以一大事因緣，出現於世。」一大事者，佛之知見也。

世人外迷著相，內迷著空。若能於相離相，於空離空，即是內外不迷。若悟此法，一念心開，是為開佛知見。

佛，猶覺也。分為四門，開覺知見，示覺知見，悟覺知見，入覺知見。若聞開示，便能悟入，即覺知見，本來真性而得出現。汝慎勿錯解經意，見他道開示悟入，自是佛之知見，我輩無分。若作此解，乃是謗經毀佛也。彼既是佛，已具知見，何用更開？汝今當信，佛知見者，只汝自心，更無別佛。

蓋為一切眾生，自蔽光明，貪愛塵境，外緣內擾，甘受驅馳。便勞他世尊，從三昧起，種種苦口，勸令寢息，莫向外求，與佛無二。故云，開佛知見。吾亦勸一切人，於自心中，常開佛之知見。

世人心邪，愚迷造罪，口善心惡，貪瞋嫉妒，諂佞我慢，侵人害物，自開眾生知見。若能正心，常生智慧，觀照自心，止惡行善，是自開佛之知見。

汝須念念開佛知見，勿開眾生知見。開佛知見，即是出世。開眾生知見，即是世間。汝若但勞勞執念，以為功課者，何異犛牛愛尾。

達曰：若然者，但得解義，不勞誦經
耶？

師曰：經有何過，豈障汝念？只為迷悟
在人，損益由己。口誦心行，即是轉
經。口誦心不行，即是被經轉。

聽吾偈曰：

> 心迷法華轉，　心悟轉法華，
> 誦經久不明，　與義作讎家。
> 無念念即正，　有念念成邪，
> 有無俱不計，　長御白牛車。

達聞偈，不覺悲泣，言下大悟，而告師
曰：法達從昔已來，實未曾轉法華，乃
被法華轉。再啟曰：經云，諸大聲聞乃
至菩薩，皆盡思共度量，不能測佛智。
今令凡夫但悟自心，便名佛之知見。自
非上根，未免疑謗。又經說三車，羊鹿
牛車與白牛之車，如何區別？願和尚再
垂開示。

師曰：經意分明，汝自迷背。諸三乘

人，不能測佛智者，患在度量也。饒伊盡思共推，轉加懸遠。佛本為凡夫說，不為佛說。此理若不肯信者，從他退席。殊不知，坐却白牛車，更於門外覓三車。況經文明向汝道，唯一佛乘，無有餘乘，若二若三。乃至無數方便，種種因緣譬喻言詞，是法皆為一佛乘故。汝何不省，三車是假，為昔時故。一乘是實，為今時故。只教汝去假歸實，歸實之後，實亦無名。應知所有珍財，盡屬於汝，由汝受用，更不作父想，亦不作子想，亦無用想。是名持法華經，從劫至劫，手不釋卷，從晝至夜，無不念時也。

達蒙啟發，踊躍歡喜，以偈讚曰：

> 經誦三千部，　曹溪一句亡，
> 未明出世旨，　寧歇累生狂。
> 羊鹿牛權設，　初中後善揚，
> 誰知火宅內，　元是法中王。

師曰：汝今後方可名念經僧也。達從此
領玄旨，亦不輟誦經。

僧智通，壽州安豐人。初看《楞伽經》
約千餘遍，而不會三身四智，禮師求解
其義。

師曰：三身者，清淨法身，汝之性也。
圓滿報身，汝之智也。千百億化身，汝
之行也。若離本性，別說三身，即名有
身無智。若悟三身無有自性，即明四智
菩提。聽吾偈曰：

> 自性具三身，　發明成四智，
> 不離見聞緣，　超然登佛地。
> 吾今為汝說，　諦信永無迷，
> 莫學馳求者，　終日說菩提。

通再啟曰：四智之義，可得聞乎？

師曰：既會三身，便明四智。何更問
耶？若離三身，別談四智，此名有智無
身。即此有智，還成無智。復說偈曰：

大圓鏡智性清淨，　平等性智心無病，
妙觀察智見非功，　成所作智同圓鏡。
五八六七果因轉，　但用名言無實性，
若於轉處不留情，　繁興永處那伽定。

(如上轉識為智也。教中云，轉前五識為成所作
智，轉第六識為妙觀察智，轉第七識為平等性
智，轉第八識為大圓鏡智。雖六七因中轉，五八
果上轉，但轉其名而不轉其體也)。

通頓悟性智，遂呈偈曰：

三身元我體，　　四智本心明，
身智融無礙，　　應物任隨形。
起修皆妄動，　　守住匪真精，
妙旨因師曉，　　終亡染污名。

僧智常，信州貴溪人，髫年出家，志求
見性。一日參禮。
師問曰：汝從何來？欲求何事？
曰：學人近往洪州白峯山禮大通和尚，
蒙示見性成佛之義。未決狐疑，遠來投
禮，伏望和尚慈悲指示。

師曰：彼有何言句？汝試舉看。

曰：智常到彼，凡經三月，未蒙示誨。為法切故，一夕獨入丈室請問，如何是某甲本心本性？大通乃曰：汝見虛空否？對曰，見。彼曰，汝見虛空有相貌否？對曰，虛空無形，有何相貌？彼曰，汝之本性，猶如虛空，了無一物可見，是名正見。無一物可知，是名真知。無有青黃長短，但見本源清淨，覺體圓明，即名見性成佛，亦名如來知見。學人雖聞此說，猶未決了，乞和尚開示。

師曰：彼師所說，猶存見知，故令汝未了。吾今示汝一偈：

　　不見一法存無見，大似浮雲遮日面，
　　不知一法守空知，還如太虛生閃電。
　　此之知見瞥然興，錯認何曾解方便，
　　汝當一念自知非，自己靈光常顯現。

常聞偈已，心意豁然。乃述偈曰：

無端起知見，　著相求菩提，
情存一念悟，　寧越昔時迷。
自性覺源體，　隨照枉遷流，
不入祖師室，　茫然趣兩頭。

智常一日問師曰：佛說三乘法，又言最
上乘。弟子未解，願為教授。

師曰：汝觀自本心，莫著外法相。法無
四乘，人心自有等差。見聞轉誦是小
乘。悟法解義是中乘。依法修行是大
乘。萬法盡通，萬法俱備，一切不染，
離諸法相，一無所得，名最上乘。乘是
行義，不在口爭。汝須自修，莫問吾
也。一切時中，自性自如。

常禮謝，執侍終師之世。

僧志道，廣州南海人也。請益曰：學人
自出家，覽《涅槃經》十載有餘，未明
大意，願和尚垂誨。師曰：汝何處未
明？曰：「諸行無常，是生滅法。生滅
滅已，寂滅為樂。」於此疑惑。

師曰：汝作麼生疑？

曰：一切眾生皆有二身，謂色身，法身
也。色身無常，有生有滅。法身有常，
無知無覺。經云「生滅滅已，寂滅為
樂」者，不審何身寂滅？何身受樂？若
色身者，色身滅時，四大分散，全然是
苦，苦不可言樂。若法身寂滅，即同草
木瓦石，誰當受樂？又法性是生滅之
體，五蘊是生滅之用，一體五用。生滅
是常，生則從體起用，滅則攝用歸體。
若聽更生，即有情之類，不斷不滅。若
不聽更生，則永歸寂滅，同於無情之
物。如是，則一切諸法被涅槃之所禁
伏，尚不得生，何樂之有？

師曰：汝是釋子，何習外道斷常邪見，
而議最上乘法？據汝所說，即色身外別
有法身，離生滅求於寂滅。又推涅槃常
樂，言有身受用。斯乃執悋生死，耽著
世樂。汝今當知，佛為一切迷人，認五
蘊和合為自體相，分別一切法為外塵

相，好生惡死，念念遷流，不知夢幻虛假，枉受輪迴。以常樂涅槃翻為苦相，終日馳求。佛愍此故，乃示涅槃真樂。剎那無有生相，剎那無有滅相，更無生滅可滅，是則寂滅現前。當現前時，亦無現前之量，乃謂常樂。此樂無有受者，亦無不受者，豈有一體五用之名？何況更言涅槃禁伏諸法，令永不生。斯乃謗佛毀法。聽吾偈曰：

> 無上大涅槃，　　圓明常寂照，
> 凡愚謂之死，　　外道執為斷，
> 諸求二乘人，　　目以為無作，
> 盡屬情所計，　　六十二見本，
> 妄立虛假名，　　何為真實義。

> 惟有過量人，　　通達無取捨，
> 以知五蘊法，　　及以蘊中我，
> 外現眾色象，　　一一音聲相，
> 平等如夢幻，　　不起凡聖見，
> 不作涅槃解，　　二邊三際斷。

常應諸根用，　　而不起用想，
分別一切法，　　不起分別想。

劫火燒海底，　　風鼓山相擊，
真常寂滅樂，　　涅槃相如是。

吾今彊言說，　　令汝捨邪見，
汝勿隨言解，　　許汝知少分。

志道聞偈大悟，踊躍作禮而退。

行思禪師，生吉州安城劉氏。聞曹溪法
席盛化，徑來參禮，遂問曰：當何所
務，即不落階級？
師曰：汝曾作什麼來？
曰：聖諦亦不為。
師曰：落何階級？
曰：聖諦尚不為，何階級之有？

師深器之，令思首眾。一日，師謂曰：
汝當分化一方，無令斷絕。
思既得法，遂回吉州青原山，弘法紹化
(諡弘濟禪師)。

懷讓禪師，金州杜氏子也。初謁嵩山安國師，安發之曹溪參扣。讓至禮拜。

師曰：甚處來？曰：嵩山。

師曰：什麼物？恁麼來？曰：說似一物即不中。

師曰：還可修證否？曰：修證即不無，污染即不得。

師曰：只此不污染，諸佛之所護念。汝既如是，吾亦如是。西天般若多羅讖，汝足下出一馬駒，踏殺天下人。應在汝心，不須速說 (一本無西天以下二十七字)。

讓豁然契會，遂執侍左右一十五載，日臻玄奧。後往南嶽，大闡禪宗 (勅諡大慧禪師)。

永嘉玄覺禪師，溫州戴氏子。少習經論，精天台止觀法門。因看《維摩經》發明心地。偶師弟子玄策相訪，與其劇談，出言暗合諸祖。策云：仁者得法師誰？曰：我聽方等經論，各有師承。後於《維摩經》悟佛心宗，未有證明者。
策云：威音王已前即得，威音王已後，
無師自悟，盡是天然外道。曰：願仁者
為我證據。策云：我言輕。曹溪有六祖
大師，四方雲集，並是受法者。若去，
則與偕行。

覺遂同策來參，繞師三匝，振錫而立。
師曰：夫沙門者，具三千威儀，八萬細
行。大德自何方而來，生大我慢？覺
曰：生死事大，無常迅速。師曰：何不
體取無生，了無速乎？曰：體即無生，
了本無速。師曰：如是，如是。

玄覺方具威儀禮拜，須臾告辭。師曰：
返太速乎？曰：本自非動，豈有速耶？
師曰：誰知非動？曰：仁者自生分別。
師曰：汝甚得無生之意。曰：無生豈有
意耶？師曰：無意，誰當分別？曰：分
別亦非意。師曰：善哉，少留一宿。時
謂一宿覺。後著《證道歌》，盛行于世
(諡曰無相大師，時稱為真覺焉)。

禪者智隍，初參五祖，自謂已得正受。菴居長坐，積二十年。師弟子玄策，游方至河朔，聞隍之名，造菴問云：汝在此作什麼？隍曰：入定。

策云：汝云入定，為有心入耶？無心入耶？若無心入者，一切無情草木瓦石，應合得定。若有心入者，一切有情含識之流，亦應得定。

隍曰：我正入定時，不見有有無之心。

策云：不見有有無之心，即是常定。何有出入？若有出入，即非大定。

隍無對，良久，問曰：師嗣誰耶？

策云：我師曹溪六祖。

隍云：六祖以何為禪定？

策云：我師所說，妙湛圓寂，體用如如。五陰本空，六塵非有，不出不入，不定不亂。禪性無住，離住禪寂。禪性無生，離生禪想。心如虛空，亦無虛空之量。隍聞是說，徑來謁師。師問云：仁者何來？隍具述前緣。師云：誠如所言。汝但心如虛空，不著空見，應用無礙，動靜無心，凡聖情忘，能所俱泯，性相如如，無不定時也 (一本無汝但以下三十五字。止云：師憫其遠來，遂垂開決)。隍於是大悟，二十年所得心，都無影響。其夜河北士庶，聞空中有聲云：隍禪師今日得道。隍後禮辭，復歸河北，開化四眾。

一僧問師云：黃梅意旨，甚麼人得？
師云：會佛法人得。
僧云：和尚還得否？
師云：我不會佛法。

師一日欲濯所授之衣而無美泉，因至寺後五里許，見山林欝茂，瑞氣盤旋。師振錫卓地，泉應手而出，積以為池，乃跪膝浣衣石上。

忽有一僧來禮拜，云：方辯是西蜀人，昨於南天竺國，見達磨大師，囑方辯速往唐土。吾傳大迦葉正法眼藏及僧伽

梨，見傳六代，於韶州曹溪，汝去瞻
禮。方辯遠來，願見我師傳來衣鉢。
師乃出示，次問：上人攻何事業？曰：
善塑。師正色曰：汝試塑看。辯罔措。
過數日，塑就真相，可高七寸，曲盡其
妙。師笑曰：汝只解塑性，不解佛性。
師舒手摩方辯頂，曰：永為人天福田。
(師仍以衣酬之。辯取衣分為三，一披塑像，一自
留，一用棕裹瘞地中。誓曰：後得此衣乃吾出世，
住持於此重建殿宇。宋嘉祐八年，有僧惟先，修殿
掘地，得衣如新。像在高泉寺，祈禱輒應)。

有僧舉臥輪禪師偈曰：

> 臥輪有伎倆，　　能斷百思想，
> 對境心不起，　　菩提日日長。

師聞之，曰：此偈未明心地，若依而行
之，是加繫縛。因示一偈曰：

> 惠能沒伎倆，　　不斷百思想，
> 對境心數起，　　菩提作麼長。

頓漸第八

時，祖師居曹溪寶林，神秀大師在荊南玉泉寺。于時兩宗盛化，人皆稱南能北秀，故有南北二宗頓漸之分，而學者莫知宗趣。師謂眾曰：法本一宗，人有南北。法即一種，見有遲疾。何名頓漸？法無頓漸，人有利鈍，故名頓漸。

然秀之徒眾，往往譏南宗祖師，不識一字，有何所長。秀曰：他得無師之智，深悟上乘。吾不如也。且吾師五祖，親傳衣法。豈徒然哉，吾恨不能遠去親近，虛受國恩。汝等諸人，毋滯於此，可往曹溪參決。一日，命門人志誠曰：汝聰明多智，可為吾到曹溪聽法。若有所聞，盡心記取，還為吾說。

志誠稟命至曹溪，隨眾參請，不言來處。時祖師告眾曰：今有盜法之人，潛在此會。志誠即出禮拜，具陳其事。

師曰：汝從玉泉來，應是細作。

對曰：不是。

師曰：何得不是？

對曰：未說即是，說了不是。

師曰：汝師若為示眾？

對曰：常指誨大眾，住心觀靜，長坐不臥。

師曰：住心觀靜，是病非禪。長坐拘身，於理何益？聽吾偈曰：

　　生來坐不臥，　　死去臥不坐，
　　一具臭骨頭，　　何為立功課？

志誠再拜曰：弟子在秀大師處，學道九年，不得契悟。今聞和尚一說，便契本心。弟子生死事大，和尚大慈，更為教示。

師云：吾聞汝師教示學人戒定慧法，未審汝師說戒定慧行相如何？與吾說看。

誠曰：秀大師說，諸惡莫作名為戒，諸善奉行名為慧，自淨其意名為定。彼說如此，未審和尚以何法誨人？

師曰：吾若言有法與人，即為誑汝。但且隨方解縛，假名三昧。如汝師所說戒定慧，實不可思議。吾所見戒定慧又別。

志誠曰：戒定慧只合一種，如何更別？

師曰：汝師戒定慧接大乘人，吾戒定慧接最上乘人。悟解不同，見有遲疾。汝聽吾說，與彼同否？吾所說法，不離自性。離體說法，名為相說，自性常迷。須知一切萬法，皆從自性起用，是真戒定慧法。聽吾偈曰：

> 心地無非自性戒，心地無癡自性慧，
> 心地無亂自性定，不增不減自金剛，
> 身去身來本三昧。

誠聞偈，悔謝，乃呈一偈曰：

> 五蘊幻身，　幻何究竟？
> 迴趣真如，　法還不淨。

師然之，復語誠曰：汝師戒定慧，勸小根智人。吾戒定慧，勸大根智人。若悟自性，亦不立菩提涅槃，亦不立解脫知見。無一法可得，方能建立萬法。若解此意，亦名佛身，亦名菩提涅槃，亦名解脫知見。見性之人，立亦得，不立亦得，去來自由，無滯無礙，應用隨作，應語隨答，普見化身，不離自性，即得自在神通，游戲三昧，是名見性。

志誠再啟師曰：如何是不立義？

師曰：自性無非，無癡無亂，念念般若觀照，常離法相，自由自在，縱橫盡得，有何可立？自性自悟，頓悟頓修，亦無漸次，所以不立一切法。諸法寂滅，有何次第？

志誠禮拜，願為執侍，朝夕不懈 (誠吉州太和人也)。

僧志徹，江西人，本姓張，名行昌，少任俠。自南北分化，二宗主雖亡彼我，而徒侶競起愛憎。時北宗門人，自立秀師為第六祖，而忌祖師傳衣為天下聞，乃囑行昌來刺師。

師心通，預知其事，即置金十兩於座間。時夜暮，行昌入祖室，將欲加害。師舒頸就之，行昌揮刃者三，悉無所損。師曰：正劍不邪，邪劍不正。只負汝金，不負汝命。

行昌驚仆，久而方蘇，求哀悔過，即願出家。師遂與金，言：汝且去，恐徒眾翻害於汝。汝可他日易形而來，吾當攝受。

行昌稟旨宵遁。後投僧出家，具戒精進。一日，憶師之言，遠來禮覲。

師曰：吾久念汝，汝來何晚？

曰：昨蒙和尚捨罪，今雖出家苦行，終難報德，其惟傳法度生乎？弟子常覽《涅槃經》，未曉常無常義。乞和尚慈悲，略為解說。

師曰：無常者，即佛性也。有常者，即一切善惡諸法分別心也。

曰：和尚所說，大違經文。

師曰：吾傳佛心印，安敢違於佛經？

曰：經說佛性是常。和尚却言無常。善惡之法乃至菩提心，皆是無常。和尚却言是常。此即相違，令學人轉加疑惑。

師曰：《涅槃經》吾昔聽尼無盡藏讀誦一遍，便為講說，無一字一義不合經文。乃至為汝，終無二說。

曰：學人識量淺昧，願和尚委曲開示。

師曰：汝知否？佛性若常，更說什麼善惡諸法，乃至窮劫，無有一人發菩提心者。故吾說無常，正是佛說真常之道也。又，一切諸法若無常者，即物物皆有自性，容受生死，而真常性有不遍之處。故吾說常者，正是佛說真無常義。佛比為凡夫，外道執於邪常，諸二乘人於常計無常，共成八倒，故於《涅槃》了義教中，破彼偏見，而顯說真常，真

樂，真我，真淨。汝今依言背義，以斷
滅無常及確定死常，而錯解佛之圓妙最
後微言。縱覽千遍，有何所益？

行昌忽然大悟，說偈曰：

　　因守無常心，　　佛說有常性，
　　不知方便者，　　猶春池拾礫。
　　我今不施功，　　佛性而現前，
　　非師相授與，　　我亦無所得。

師曰：汝今徹也，宜名志徹。徹禮謝而
退。

有一童子，名神會，襄陽高氏子。年十
三，自玉泉來參禮。
師曰：知識遠來艱辛，還將得本來否？
若有本則合識主。試說看。
會曰：以無住為本，見即是主。
師曰：這沙彌爭合取次語？
會乃問曰：和尚坐禪，還見不見？
師以柱杖打三下，云：吾打汝痛不痛？

對曰：亦痛亦不痛。

師曰：吾亦見亦不見。

神會問：如何是亦見亦不見？

師云：吾之所見，常見自心過愆，不見他人是非好惡，是以亦見亦不見。汝言亦痛亦不痛。如何？汝若不痛，同其木石。若痛，則同凡夫，即起恚恨。汝向前見不見是二邊，痛不痛是生滅。汝自性且不見，敢爾弄人，神會禮拜悔謝。

師又曰：汝若心迷不見，問善知識覓路。汝若心悟，即自見性依法修行。汝自迷不見自心，却來問吾見與不見。吾見自知，豈代汝迷？汝若自見，亦不代吾迷。何不自知自見，乃問吾見與不見？

神會再禮百餘拜，求謝過愆。服勤給侍，不離左右。

一日，師告眾曰：吾有一物，無頭無尾，無名無字，無背無面。諸人還識否？神會出曰：是諸佛之本源，神會之佛性。師曰：向汝道，無名無字，汝便喚作本源佛性。汝向去有把茆蓋頭，也只成箇知解宗徒。

祖師滅後，會入京洛，大弘曹溪頓教，著《顯宗記》，盛行于世 (是為荷澤禪師)。

師見諸宗難問咸起惡心，多集座下愍而謂曰：學道之人，一切善念惡念應當盡除。無名可名，名於自性，無二之性，是名實性。於實性上建立一切教門，言下便須自見。

諸人聞說，總皆作禮，請事為師。

宣詔第九

神龍元年上元日，則天．中宗詔云：
朕請安．秀二師宮中供養。萬機之暇，
每究一乘。二師推讓云，南方有能禪
師，密授忍大師衣法，傳佛心印，可請
彼問。今遣內侍薛簡，馳詔迎請，願師
慈念，速赴上京。

師上表辭疾，願終林麓。

薛簡曰：京城禪德皆云：欲得會道，必
須坐禪習定。若不因禪定而得解脫者，
未之有也。未審師所說法如何？

師曰：道由心悟，豈在坐也。經云：若
言如來若坐若臥，是行邪道。何故？無
所從來，亦無所去。無生無滅，是如來
清淨禪。諸法空寂，是如來清淨坐。究
竟無證，豈況坐耶。

簡曰：弟子回京，主上必問。願師慈
悲，指示心要，傳奏兩宮及京城學道

者。譬如一燈，然百千燈，冥者皆明，明明無盡。

師云：道無明暗，明暗是代謝之義。明明無盡，亦是有盡，相待立名故。

《淨名經》云：法無有比，無相待故。

簡曰：明喻智慧，暗喻煩惱。修道之人，倘不以智慧照破煩惱，無始生死憑何出離？

師曰：煩惱即是菩提，無二無別。若以智慧照破煩惱者，此是二乘見解。羊鹿等機，上智大根，悉不如是。

簡曰：如何是大乘見解？

師曰：明與無明，凡夫見二。智者了達，其性無二。無二之性，即是實性。實性者，處凡愚而不減，在賢聖而不增，住煩惱而不亂，居禪定而不寂。不斷不常，不來不去，不在中間及其內外，不生不滅，性相如如，常住不遷，名之曰道。

簡曰：師說不生不滅，何異外道？

師曰：外道所說不生不滅者，將滅止生，以生顯滅，滅猶不滅，生說不生。我說不生不滅者，本自無生，今亦不滅，所以不同外道。汝若欲知心要，但一切善惡都莫思量，自然得入清淨心體，湛然常寂，妙用恒沙。

簡蒙指教，豁然大悟。禮辭歸闕，表奏師語。

其年九月三日，有詔獎諭師曰：師辭老疾，為朕修道，國之福田。師若淨名托疾毘耶，闡揚大乘，傳諸佛心，談不二法。薛簡傳師指授如來知見，朕積善餘慶，宿種善根，值師出世，頓悟上乘。感荷師恩，頂戴無已，并奉磨衲袈裟及水晶鉢，勅韶州刺史修飾寺宇，賜師舊居為國恩寺。

付囑第十

師一日喚門人法海，志誠，法達，神會，智常，智通，志徹，志道，法珍，法如等，曰：汝等不同餘人，吾滅度後，各為一方師。吾今教汝說法，不失本宗。先須舉三科法門，動用三十六對，出沒即離兩邊。說一切法，莫離自性。忽有人問汝法，出語盡雙，皆取對法，來去相因。究竟二法盡除，更無去處。

三科法門者，陰界入也。陰是五陰，色受想行識是也。入是十二入。外六塵，色聲香味觸法。內六門，眼耳鼻舌身意是也。界是十八界，六塵，六門，六識是也。

自性能含萬法，名含藏識。若起思量，即是轉識。生六識，出六門，見六塵。如是一十八界，皆從自性起用。自性若邪，起十八邪。自性若正，起十八正。

若惡用即眾生用，善用即佛用。用由何等？由自性有。

對法，外境無情五對。天與地對，日與月對，明與暗對，陰與陽對，水與火對。此是五對也。

法相語言十二對。語與法對，有與無對，有色與無色對，有相與無相對，有漏與無漏對，色與空對，動與靜對，清與濁對，凡與聖對，僧與俗對，老與少對，大與小對。此是十二對也。

自性起用十九對。長與短對，邪與正對，癡與慧對，愚與智對，亂與定對，慈與毒對，戒與非對，直與曲對，實與虛對，險與平對，煩惱與菩提對，常與無常對，悲與害對，喜與瞋對，捨與慳對，進與退對，生與滅對，法身與色身對，化身與報身對。此是十九對也。

師言：此三十六對法，若解用即道，貫

一切經法，出入即離兩邊。自性動用，共人言語，外於相離相，內於空離空。若全著相，即長邪見。若全執空，即長無明。執空之人有謗經，直言不用文字。既云不用文字，人亦不合語言。只此語言，便是文字之相。又云，直道不立文字。即此不立兩字，亦是文字。見人所說，便即謗他言著文字。汝等須知，自迷猶可，又謗佛經。不要謗經，罪障無數。

若著相於外，而作法求真。或廣立道場，說有無之過患。如是之人，累劫不得見性。但聽依法修行，又莫百物不思，而於道性窒礙。若聽說不修，令人反生邪念。但依法修行，無住相法施。汝等若悟，依此說，依此用，依此行，依此作，即不失本宗。

若有人問汝義，問有將無對，問無將有對。問凡以聖對，問聖以凡對。二道相因，生中道義。如一問一對，餘問一依此作，即不失理也。設有人問，何名為闇？答云，明是因，闇是緣，明沒即闇。以明顯闇，以闇顯明，來去相因，成中道義。餘問悉皆如此。汝等於後傳法，依此轉相教授，勿失宗旨。

師於太極元年壬子，延和七月(是年五月改延和，八月玄宗即位方改元先天，次年遂改開元。他本作先天者非) 命門人往新州國恩寺建塔，仍令促工，次年夏末落成。

七月一日，集徒眾曰：吾至八月，欲離世間。汝等有疑，早須相問，為汝破疑，令汝迷盡。吾若去後，無人教汝。

法海等聞，悉皆涕泣。惟有神會，神情不動，亦無涕泣。

師云：神會小師却得善不善等，毀譽不動，哀樂不生。餘者不得。數年山中，竟修何道？汝今悲泣，為憂阿誰？若憂

吾不知去處，吾自知去處。吾若不知去
處，終不預報於汝。汝等悲泣，蓋為不
知吾去處。若知吾去處，即不合悲泣。
法性本無生滅去來，汝等盡坐，吾與汝
說一偈，名曰真假動靜偈。汝等誦取此
偈，與吾意同，依此修行，不失宗旨。
眾僧作禮，請師說偈。偈曰：

> 一切無有真，　不以見於真，
> 若見於真者，　是見盡非真。

> 若能自有真，　離假即心真，
> 自心不離假，　無真何處真？

> 有情即解動，　無情即不動，
> 若修不動行，　同無情不動。

> 若覓真不動，　動上有不動，
> 不動是不動，　無情無佛種。

> 能善分別相，　第一義不動，
> 但作如此見，　即是真如用。

報諸學道人，　努力須用意，
莫於大乘門，　却執生死智。

若言下相應，　即共論佛義，
若實不相應，　合掌令歡喜。

此宗本無諍，　諍即失道意，
執逆諍法門，　自性入生死。

時，徒眾聞說偈已，普皆作禮，並體師意，各各攝心，依法修行，更不敢諍。

乃知大師不久住世，法海上座，再拜問曰：和尚入滅之後，衣法當付何人？

師曰：吾於大梵寺說法，以至于今抄錄流行，目曰“法寶壇經”。汝等守護，遞相傳授。度諸群生，但依此說，是名正法。

今為汝等說法，不付其衣。蓋為汝等信根淳熟，決定無疑，堪任大事。然據先祖達磨大師付授偈意，衣不合傳。

偈曰:

> 吾本來茲土，　傳法救迷情，
> 一華開五葉，　結果自然成。

師復曰: 諸善知識，汝等各各淨心，聽吾說法。若欲成就種智，須達相三昧，一行三昧。

若於一切處而不住相，於彼相中不生憎愛，亦無取捨，不念利益成壞等事，安閒恬靜，虛融澹泊，此名一相三昧。

若於一切處行住坐臥，純一直心，不動道場，真成淨土，此名一行三昧。

若人具二三昧，如地有種，含藏長養，成熟其實。一相一行，亦復如是。

我今說法，猶如時雨，普潤大地。汝等佛性，譬諸種子，遇茲霑洽，悉得發生。承吾旨者，決獲菩提。依吾行者，定證妙果。聽吾偈曰:

心地含諸種， 普雨悉皆萌，
頓悟華情已， 菩提果自成。

師說偈已，曰：其法無二，其心亦然。
其道清淨，亦無諸相，汝等慎勿觀靜及
空其心。此心本淨，無可取捨。各自努
力，隨緣好去。

爾時徒眾作禮而退。

大師，七月八日忽謂門人曰：吾欲歸新
州，汝等速理舟楫。大眾哀留甚堅。

師曰：諸佛出現，猶示涅槃。有來必
去，理亦常然。吾此形骸，歸必有所。

眾曰：師從此去，早晚可回。
師曰：葉落歸根，來時無口。

又問曰：正法眼藏，傳付何人？
師曰：有道者得，無心者通。

又問：後莫有難否？
師曰：吾滅後五六年，當有一人來取吾

首。聽吾記曰：

頭上養親，　　口裏須餐，
遇滿之難，　　楊柳為官。

又云：吾去七十年，有二菩薩從東方來，一山家，一在家。同時興化，建立吾宗，締緝伽藍，昌隆法嗣。

問曰：未知從上佛祖應現已來，傳授幾代？願垂開示。

師云：古佛應世已無數量，不可計也。今以七佛為始，過去莊嚴劫，毘婆尸佛，尸棄佛，毘舍浮佛。今賢劫，拘留孫佛，拘那含牟尼佛，迦葉佛，釋迦文佛。是為七佛。

已上七佛。今以釋迦文佛，首傳第一摩訶迦葉尊者，第二阿難尊者，第三商那和修尊者，第四優波毱多尊者，第五提多迦尊者，第六彌遮迦尊者，第七婆須蜜多尊者，第八佛馱難提尊者，第九伏馱蜜多尊者，第十脇尊者，十一富那夜奢尊者，十二馬鳴大士，十三迦毘摩羅尊者，十四龍樹大士，十五迦那提婆尊者，十六羅睺羅多尊者，十七僧伽難提尊者，十八伽耶舍多尊者，十九鳩摩羅多尊者，二十闍耶多尊者，二十一婆修盤頭尊者，二十二摩拏羅尊者，二十三鶴勒那尊者，二十四師子尊者，二十五婆舍斯多尊者，二十六不如蜜多尊者，二十七般若多羅尊者，二十八菩提達磨尊者 (此土是為初祖)，二十九慧可大師，三十僧璨大師，三十一道信大師，三十二弘忍大師。惠能是為三十三祖。

從上諸祖，各有稟承。汝等向後，遞代流傳，毋令乖誤。

大師，先天二年癸丑歲八月初三日 (是年十二月改元開元)，於國恩寺齋罷，謂諸徒眾曰：汝等各依位坐，吾與汝別。

法海白言：和尚，留何教法，令後代迷

人，得見佛性？

師言：汝等諦聽，後代迷人，若識眾生，即是佛性。若不識眾生，萬劫覓佛難逢。吾今教汝。識自心眾生，見自心佛性。欲求見佛，但識眾生。只為眾生迷佛，非是佛迷眾生。

自性若悟，眾生是佛。自性若迷，佛是眾生。自性平等，眾生是佛。自性邪險，佛是眾生。汝等心若險曲，即佛在眾生中。一念平直。即是眾生成佛。

我心自有佛，自佛是真佛。自若無佛心，何處求真佛？

汝等自心是佛，更莫狐疑。外無一物而能建立，皆是本心生萬種法。故經云，心生種種法生，心滅種種法滅。

吾今留一偈與汝等別，名自性真佛偈。後代之人，識此偈意，自見本心，自成佛道。偈曰：

真如自性是真佛，邪見三毒是魔王，
邪迷之時魔在舍，正見之時佛在堂。

性中邪見三毒生，即是魔王來住舍，
正見自除三毒心，魔變成佛真無假。

法身報身及化身，三身本來是一身，
若向性中能自見，即是成佛菩提因。

本從化身生淨性，淨性常在化身中，
性使化身行正道，當來圓滿真無窮。

婬性本是淨性因，除婬即是淨性身，
性中各自離五欲，見性剎那即是真。

今生若遇頓教門，忽悟自性見世尊，
若欲修行覓作佛，不知何處擬求真？

若能心中自見真，有真即是成佛因，
不見自性外覓佛，起心總是大癡人。

頓教法門今已留，救度世人須自修，
報汝當來學道者，不作此見大悠悠。

師說偈已，告曰：汝等好住。吾滅度
後，莫作世情，悲泣雨淚，受人弔問，
身著孝服，非吾弟子，亦非正法。

但識自本心，見自本性，無動無靜，無
生無滅，無去無來，無是無非，無住無
往。恐汝等心迷，不會吾意，今再囑
汝，令汝見性。吾滅度後，依此修行，
如吾在日。若違吾教，縱吾在世，亦無
有益。復說偈曰：

> 兀兀不修善，　騰騰不造惡，
> 寂寂斷見聞，　蕩蕩心無著。

師說偈已，端坐至三更，忽謂門人曰：
吾行矣。

奄然遷化。于時異香滿室，白虹屬地，
林木變白，禽獸哀鳴。

十一月，廣韶新三郡官僚，洎門人僧
俗，爭迎真身，莫決所之。乃焚香禱
曰：香煙指處，師所歸焉。時香煙直貫

曹溪。十一月十三日,遷神龕併所傳衣鉢而回。次年七月出龕,弟子方辯以香泥上之,門人憶念取首之記,仍以鐵葉漆布固護師頸入塔。忽於塔內白光出現,直上衝天,三日始散。韶州奏聞,奉勅立碑,紀師道行。

師春秋七十有六,年二十四傳衣,三十九祝髮,說法利生三十七載,嗣法四十三人,悟道超凡者莫知其數。達磨所傳信衣 (西域屈眴布也),中宗賜磨衲寶鉢,及方辯塑師真相,并道具,永鎮寶林道場。留傳《壇經》以顯宗旨,興隆三寶,普利群生者。

六祖大師法寶壇經(終)

The Sixth Patriarch's Sutra is set in 12½ Garamond Premier Pro,
a face designed for photocomposition by Robert Slimbach
and modeled after the roman types of Claude Garamond
and the italic types of Robert Granjon. The sans serif
is 10½ Myriad Pro, a humanist typeface designed by
Robert Slimbach and Carol Twombly. The Chinese
display characters that accompany the images of
the Patriarchs are 50 and 60 Biau Kai.
The Chinese Sutra is set in 18 Adobe Song.

DESIGN AND COMPOSITION: Classic Typography

PRINTED BY Data Reproductions Corporation
on 55 lb. Natural Antique

BINDERY: Dekker Book Binding.
Smyth sewn case binding with
Arlington Vellum Royal cloth